1988 Project Series
No. 2

Human Rights and
U.S. Foreign Polic'

WORKER RIGHTS UNDER THE U.S. TRADE LAWS

Lawyers Committee for Human Rights
330 Seventh Avenue, 10th Floor
New York, New York 10001
(212) 629-6170
FAX: (212) 967-0916

Printed in the United States of America

The Lawyers Committee for Human Rights

Since 1978 the Lawyers Committee has served as a public interest law center. The Lawyers Committee works to promote international human rights law and legal procedures in the United States and abroad. The chairman of the Lawyers Committee is Marvin E. Frankel; Michael H. Posner is its Executive Director. The 1988 Project was coordinated by Roger L. Waldman, a partner at Webster & Sheffield, and at the Lawyers Committee, by Patricia Armstrong. This report is part of the 1988 Project Series. Those wishing copies of other reports in the series should contact the Lawyers Committee.

Copies of this report are available from:

Lawyers Committee for Human Rights
330 Seventh Avenue, 10th Floor
New York, New York 10001

ISBN # 0-934143-22-6

TABLE OF CONTENTS

Preface v

Lawyers Committee Recommendations vii

EXECUTIVE SUMMARY 1

I. INTRODUCTION 9

II. THE UNITED STATES' PREFERENTIAL DUTY PROGRAMS 11

A. The Generalized System of Preferences 11

1. The GSP's Worker Rights Provision 13

2. Administration of the Worker Rights Provision 17

a. Petitioning the Trade Policy Staff Committee on Worker Rights Violations During the GSP Annual Review 20

b. The Annual Review Process 21

c. Substantive Standards Governing the Consideration of Worker Rights Petitions 24

(1) Standards Applied in Phase One Determinations 25

(2) Standards Applied in Phase Two Determinations 26

(3) Factors Supporting the President's Termination of GSP Benefits to Nicaragua, Paraguay, Romania and Chile 30

d. The Burden of Persuasion Imposed In Review Proceedings 32

e. Conclusion 33

B. The Caribbean Basin Initiative 33

C. The Efficacy of Using Preferential Duty Programs as Leverage to Promote Worker Rights Abroad 35

D. Options to Improve the Efficacy of the Preferential Duty Programs 42

1. Information Gathering and Resource Development 42

2. Procedural Reforms Concerning the GSP Annual Review Process 43

a. Clarify the GSP Regulation 43

b. Formalize the Procedures by Which the USTR Publicizes the Determinations of the President Following Worker Rights Review Proceedings 44

c. Provide for Increased Public Participation in the Review Process 44

d. Relocate the Decisionmaking Authority . 45

3. Substantive Reforms Concerning the Administration of the GSP Program 45

a. Review the Worker Rights Practices of All Beneficiary Developing Countries 45

b. Broaden the Scope of Violations That Could Result in Termination from the GSP Program 46

c. Reconsider the Reagan Administration's Decisions in Certain Previous Reviews 46

4. Review of CBI Beneficiaries 47

5. A Refined Approach to Preferential Duty Programs and Worker Rights 47

III. SECTION 301 OF THE TRADE ACT OF 1974 51

A. The President's Authority under Section 301 53

1. Mandatory Action 53

2. Discretionary Authority to Respond to the Denial of Internationally Recognized Worker Rights and Other Unfair Trade Practices 55

B. Procedures for Review of Unfair Trade Practices (Including the Denial of Internationally Recognized Worker Rights) under Section 301 57

1. Initiation of Investigations 58

2. Consultation and Referral Upon Initiation of Investigation 59

3. Final Determinations by the USTR 61

C. Retaliatory Trade Measures Authorized by Section 301 62

D. Potential Problems with the Enforcement of the Worker Rights Provision of Section 301 63

1. Inconsistency with United States Obligations under the General Agreement on Tariffs and Trade 64

2. Difficulties in Quantifying the Burden on U.S. Commerce 67

3. Confrontational Nature of Section 301 Proceedings 69

E. Conclusion and Recommendations 69

1. Enhanced Opportunities for Bilateral Negotiation Efforts 70

2. Domestic Negotiations and Agreements 71

3. Public Relations-Based Incentives to Improve Worker Rights Practices 72

4. Making an Example of Egregious Violators 72

IV. THE INTERNATIONAL EMERGENCY ECONOMIC POWERS ACT 74

A. The President's Authority Under the International Emergency Economic Powers Act 74

B. The South African Sanctions 74

C. Conclusion and Recommendations 76

PREFACE

This is one of a series of papers drawn from memoranda prepared as part of the 1988 Project, a review of human rights and U.S. foreign policy issues undertaken in 1988 by the Lawyers Committee for Human Rights. The Committee is a ten-year-old non-governmental human rights organization. The ultimate purpose of the Project was to identify specific and practical recommendations for Executive and Congressional policymakers in each of fourteen topic areas. The first and in many respects most important phase of the review process was the preparation of detailed memoranda by some of America's most respected law firms. These memos provided the basis for a series of meetings of experts in October during which a range of policy options was discussed. In December 1988, the Lawyers Committee issued a report entitled *1988 Project - Human Rights and U.S. Foreign Policy* in which it made more than 100 recommendations for action. Copies of this report are available from the Lawyers Committee.

While we have fulfilled the original purpose of the Project, we believe that the memoranda prepared can make a useful contribution to the ongoing debate on the policies and programs that the United States should be pursuing into the 1990s. We will therefore be publishing a number of these memos in the coming months.

The paper presented here reviews four recent U.S. laws that link foreign trade with worker rights protection in exporting countries and analyzes various strategies and recommendations for future action. This paper was authored for the Lawyers Committee by Bruce H. Turnbull, a partner at the firm of Weil, Gotshal & Manges, Washington, D.C., and Ethan S. Naftalin (summer associate and law clerk, J.D. expected

1989, Georgetown University Law Center). It was completed in the fall of 1988. The Lawyers Committee is extremely grateful to them for their time and commitment to this project.

The Lawyers Committee for Human Rights

New York, New York
March, 1989

LAWYERS COMMITTEE RECOMMENDATIONS

In its report *1988 Project: Human Rights and U.S. Foreign Policy,* the Lawyers Committee made the following recommendations regarding the worker rights provisions of U.S. law and their implementation:

A. Executive Branch Initiatives

1. The President should take steps to increase the ability of the United States to monitor worker rights practices abroad by (a) establishing a separate investigative unit within the Labor Department to conduct field research and (b) adding labor attachés to embassies where no such positions exist and where countries have poor or marginal worker rights records.

2. The U.S. Trade Representative should amend regulations governing the Generalized System of Preferences (GSP) and the Caribbean Basin Initiative (CBI) programs to provide that:

a. violations of human rights that interfere with worker rights shall be violations of worker rights for purposes of trade preference programs;

b. the worker rights practices of all countries receiving benefits under either program shall be subject to periodic review whether or not a petition seeking such review has been filed;

c. petitions containing a *prima facie* case of a violation of worker rights shall be accepted for review;

d. the legal and factual basis for decisions regarding both the initial rejection of petitions and the ultimate outcome of a review shall be explained and published, including the complaints sustained and the demands made upon the beneficiary country by the U.S. Trade Representative, with non-confidential material submitted in connection with the review available for inspection; and

e. the review process shall permit increased public participation in order to maximize public awareness of worker rights conditions arising from the review process.

3. To increase its ability to accurately review worker rights practices abroad, the USTR should draw upon the expertise and resources of the international labor and human rights communities.

4. The USTR should monitor compliance with pledges regarding worker rights made by countries in the CBI Program as a condition to their being designated beneficiaries. Countries that have not made promised progress in the area of worker rights should lose their preferential status.

B. Congressional Initiatives

1. In connection with the GSP Program, Congress should pass legislation to clarify what constitutes "taking steps" to afford rights to workers.

2. To the extent Recommendations A. 1 and 2 are not adopted by the Executive Branch, Congress should adopt appropriate legislation to require the addition of the described positions and procedural protections.

WORKER RIGHTS UNDER THE U.S. TRADE LAWS*

EXECUTIVE SUMMARY

Worker Rights and the U.S. Preferential Duty Programs

Under recent amendments to the legislation governing the United States' preferential duty programs, the U.S. Congress has sought to revoke trade benefits to foreign countries whose governments deny fundamental worker rights to their citizens. These amendments condition foreign country participation in the Generalized System of Preferences (GSP) and Caribbean Basin Initiative (CBI) programs on their governments' provision of five internationally recognized worker rights including the right of association, the right to organize and bargain collectively, a prohibition on the use of any form of forced or compulsory labor, a minimum age for the employment of children, and acceptable conditions of work with respect to minimum wages, hours of work, and occupational safety and health.

The purpose of this legislation is threefold: 1) to provide an opportunity for the United States government to develop and use its leverage to promote respect for worker rights abroad, 2) to allow the United States to take a moral stand against certain foreign governments that commit egregious human rights and worker rights violations, and 3) to offset the unfair trade advantage obtained by foreign countries whose governments deny or restrict fundamental worker rights. While the linkage of United States market access with acceptable worker rights practices is a contentious issue between the United States and many of its trading partners, the worker rights provisions of the GSP and CBI statutes are consistent with the United States' obligations under the General Agreement on Tariffs and Trade (GATT).

The President enforces the GSP's worker rights provision primarily through Annual Reviews conducted by the GSP

---

*. This paper is part of a book being prepared for the Pennsylvania Studies in Human Rights published by the University of Pennsylvania Press.

Subcommittee of the Trade Policy Staff Committee, an interagency group representing the Departments of State, Labor, Agriculture, Commerce and Treasury, as well as the United States Trade Representative (USTR). During the Annual Review process, the GSP Subcommittee accepts worker rights petitions from interested parties, usually labor and human rights organizations, seeking the removal of certain designated beneficiary developing countries for worker rights violations.

A worker rights petition is reviewed by the Trade Policy Staff Committee in two phases. In Phase One, the agency determines whether the petition meets the regulatory standards for review. Normally a petition will be accepted unless it is facially deficient or the petitioners fail to present substantial new information concerning a beneficiary country's worker rights practices that have previously been reviewed by the Committee. In Phase Two, the Committee reviews the merits of the petition and investigates the labor practices of the country at issue. Following the Review, the full Committee makes recommendations to the President concerning the disposition of the case. To date, the President has removed or suspended four countries from the GSP program due to worker rights violations: Chile, Nicaragua, Paraguay and Romania. The legal and factual bases for these and other worker rights determinations remain unclear since the Administration has yet to promulgate a comprehensive regulation governing the adjudication of worker rights petitions and since the USTR does not publish extensive opinions concerning the disposition of individual cases.

The CBI program has a worker rights provision similar to that of the GSP program. Unlike the GSP program, however, the CBI program does not include periodic reviews of worker rights practices of the beneficiary countries. No beneficiary developing country otherwise eligible for participation in the CBI program has ever been denied CBI benefits due to worker rights violations.

While the efficacy of preferential duty programs in promoting worker rights is limited by the extent of the trade benefits they can provide, these programs nonetheless offer the next Administration a considerable opportunity to use the United States' diplomatic and economic leverage to advance worker rights in many countries interested in maintaining favorable relations with the United States.

The administration of the worker rights provisions of the GSP and CBI programs could be improved in several ways by the next Administration:

* Increasing the United States' ability to monitor the provision of worker rights abroad by drawing on the expertise and resources of the international labor and human rights community and by allocating additional resources to the administrative bodies that currently monitor labor rights abroad.

* Revising or supplementing the current GSP regulations to clarify the procedures the Trade Policy Staff Committee must follow as well as the standards the agency must apply in conducting worker rights reviews during the Annual Review process.

* Directing the Trade Policy Staff Committee to review the worker rights practices of *all* countries receiving preferential duty treatment under both the GSP and CBI programs, not merely those countries against whom worker rights petitions have been filed.

* Placing the burden of persuasion with regard to the provision of worker rights on the beneficiary countries and not upon the worker rights petitioners.

* Amending the GSP regulation to allow for increased public participation during all stages of the Annual Review process (e.g. maintaining a non-confidential version of the agency record in each investigation that would be open for public inspection and comment) to maximize the public relations benefits arising from the review process.

* Considering the removal of authority for making worker rights recommendations from the Trade Policy Staff Committee to either the Department of State or the Department of Labor since those agencies have traditionally been more knowledgeable about and sensitive

to worker rights and human rights than the various trade agencies.

* Asking the Congress to amend the GSP and CBI statutes to include the denial of *human* rights as a basis for the denial of preferential duty treatment under the two programs.

* Reconsidering several of the Reagan Administration's previous worker rights decisions on the merits of each case.

Promotion of Worker Rights under Section 301 of the Trade Act of 1974 and the International Emergency Economic Powers Act

The President of the United States currently has the authority under two federal statutes to impose severe trade sanctions against foreign countries whose governments are found to deny internationally recognized worker rights to their citizens. The first law, Section 301 of the Trade Act of 1974 (Section 301), was recently amended by the Omnibus Trade and Competitiveness Act of 1988 to confer broad discretionary authority upon the President to impose retaliatory duties upon or to deny U.S. market access to the products of foreign countries found to deny worker rights. The President holds similar authority under the International Emergency Economic Powers Act, enacted in 1977. The invocation of executive authority under either statute, however, raises serious issues concerning the United States' obligations under the major multilateral agreement governing world trade.

The rationale behind the worker rights amendments to Section 301 parallels that behind the worker rights provisions of the United States' preferential duty programs discussed above. The worker rights provision of Section 301 provides the U.S. government an opportunity to develop and use its leverage to promote respect for worker rights abroad. Further, it allows the United States to take a moral stand against certain foreign governments that commit egregious human rights and worker rights violations. Finally, and perhaps most importantly to the American labor community, Section 301 gives the President the means with which to offset the unfair cost advantage obtained by foreign producers whose governments deny or restrict fundamental worker rights.

As in the case of the preferential duty programs, the worker rights provisions of Section 301 will be administered by the USTR. Under Section 301, the President at his discretion may unilaterally impose trade sanctions against the products of another country if the USTR finds that the government of that country is engaging in a persistent pattern of conduct that denies its workers internationally recognized worker rights. Section 301's definition of internationally recognized worker rights is identical to that contained in the preferential duty programs discussed above.

Since the worker rights amendments to Section 301 have only been in effect for a short time, there is no administrative record regarding worker rights investigations to review in this memorandum. Under the Omnibus Trade Act, however, worker rights reviews would be conducted by the USTR under the same procedures as those involving reviews of other unfair trade practices.

The application of Section 301 to unfair trade practices by foreign governments normally entails a lengthy administrative proceeding conducted by the USTR. The Section 301 process involves investigation, consultation, negotiation with the foreign government involved, referral to the dispute resolution process of the major multilateral agreement governing world trade, if applicable, and, if such efforts fail, a recommendation to the President from the USTR concerning what trade sanctions, if any, should be imposed against the foreign government. Most disputes involving Section 301 are resolved through negotiation, and the actual imposition of trade sanctions under this statute is uncommon.

If the USTR were to initiate a worker rights proceeding under Section 301, the matter would be referred to bilateral negotiations between the United States and the foreign government involved. If the negotiations do not lead to a resolution of the dispute (*i.e.* an agreement on the part of the respondent to improve its worker rights practices) and the USTR were to make a final determination that the foreign government was denying internationally recognized worker rights to its citizens, the President at his discretion could impose retaliatory trade sanctions against products from that country. These could include the imposition of additional customs duties on such products or the complete denial of U.S. market access to such goods or services originating in the subject country. The President need not retaliate in any given case if he finds that the foreign government under review has taken substantial steps toward affording workers in that country the enumerated rights or if the conditions of labor there are consistent with that country's level of economic development.

The application of Section 301 to the denial of worker rights abroad raises serious issues of international law and administrative practicability. The actual imposition of trade sanctions against a foreign country due to worker rights violations under Section 301 would likely fun afoul of GATT if the respondent country in the case were a GATT signatory. GATT's most-favored-nation (MFN) clause imposes the duty of non-discriminatory trade and tariff treatment upon each signatory with respect to the goods from all other signatories; GATT does not currently recognize the denial of worker rights as an exception to the MFN rule. If a GATT review panel were to conclude that the United States had unlawfully breached the MFN clause by imposing worker rights-related trade sanctions against a fellow signatory, the United States could eventually be subject to lawful trade retaliation by other GATT signatories. The imposition of trade sanctions in response to a worker rights petition would also create administrative difficulties in quantifying the burden to U.S. commerce created by foreign labor practices. Some Reagan Administration critics of the worker rights amendments also charged that the confrontational nature of Section 301 proceedings would preclude any constructive results arising from this process.

While these concerns necessitate considerable restraint in the application of Section 301 to worker rights violations, they do not completely rule out the successful employment of the new worker rights provision. The next Administration could take advantage of the new worker rights amendment in several ways by:

* Using the President's inherent negotiating authority as well as that provided by Section 301 to enter into substantive negotiations with the United States' major trading partners, particularly in Asia. Such negotiations would be directed at reaching bilateral trade agreement concerning the provisions of worker rights abroad. These agreements would be enforceable directly under Section 301.

* Negotiating with the domestic U.S. wholesaling and retailing communities to arrive at federally sanctioned covenants not to purchase goods from countries that violate fundamental worker rights.

* Initiating worker rights review proceedings under Section 301 against those countries (including GATT signatories) likely to respond constructively to the adverse publicity surrounding such investigations.

* Making an example of egregious worker rights violators by imposing actual trade sanctions under Section 301. Many of the world's worst violators, such as Paraguay, are not GATT signatories, and therefore not entitled to MFN treatment under the Agreement.

The International Emergency Economic Powers Act (IEEPA) authorizes the President to impose virtually unlimited trade sanctions against any other country in times of national emergency. The President may invoke his IEEPA powers only by declaring a national emergency with respect to an "unusual and extraordinary threat" to the national security, foreign policy, or economy of the United States. Although the IEEPA was not enacted as a labor rights statute, the Reagan Administration imposed trade sanctions against South Africa under this law in 1986 partly in response to that country's denial of worker rights.

The IEEPA statute is technically written so as to fall within the national security exception to GATT's MFN requirement as provided for by Article 21 of GATT. Whether the routine imposition of worker rights-related IEEPA sanctions against GATT signatories could withstand GATT scrutiny is an open question. No provision of U.S. or international law, however, appears to preclude the imposition of IEEPA sanctions against a country that is not a GATT signatory.

of IEEPA sanctions against a country that is not a GATT signatory.

Conclusion

The recent worker rights amendments to the U.S. trade laws create opportunities for the United States to develop and use its leverage on several levels to promote respect for worker rights abroad. While a small number of the United States' trading partners should be completely removed from the preferential duty programs and denied other trade benefits due to atrocious human rights and worker rights violations, the majority of foreign countries with worker rights deficiencies show the potential for improvement in this area if the United States is willing to apply aggressively its political, diplomatic, and economic leverage on this issue. The worker rights provisions of the preferential duty programs and Section 301 offer an excellent forum and considerable flexibility toward promoting these objectives.

WORKER RIGHTS UNDER THE U.S. TRADE LAWS

I. INTRODUCTION

This memorandum reviews the recently-enacted United States laws that link foreign trade with worker rights protection in exporting countries. The scope of this review includes the United States' preferential duty programs (the Generalized System of Preferences and the Caribbean Basin Initiative) as well as Section 301 of the Trade Act of 1974 and the International Emergency Economic Powers Act. The paper devotes particular attention to current administrative practice regarding the enforcement of these laws and recommends strategies and reforms by which the efficacy of these measures could be enhanced to promote worker rights.

The federal government has recently begun to address the denial of internationally recognized worker rights to foreign workers producing articles for export to the United States. Respect for worker rights varies considerably among the United States' trading partners. In recent years, foreign governments in countries such as Chile, Paraguay, Taiwan, El Salvador, Haiti, and Romania have repeatedly faced allegations of widespread worker rights violations. In addition to the concern over the rights of foreign workers, it is also widely viewed in the United States that the denial of fundamental rights to workers abroad creates an unfair cost advantage in favor of the foreign goods that are produced under repressive conditions and these practices threaten the economic well-being of workers and responsible employers in the United States.[1]

U.S. concern over worker rights has recently led to import trade legislation that could limit access to U.S. markets or U.S. trade benefits for countries found to deny fundamental worker rights to their citizens. The rationale behind this legislation is threefold. First, these laws provide an opportunity for the

---

1. *Workers' Rights and Trade Adjustment Assistance Programs: Hearing on S. 490 and H.R. 3 Before the Sen. Comm. on Finance,* 100th Cong., 1st Sess. 38 (1987) (statement of Rep. Donald J. Pease) [hereinafter *Senate Workers' Rights Hearing*].

United States government to develop and use its political, economic and diplomatic leverage to promote respect for worker rights abroad. Second, the legislation allows the United States to take a moral stand against certain foreign governments that commit egregious human rights and worker rights violations. Finally, the legislation allows the U.S. Government to offset some of the unfair trade advantage obtained by producers in foreign countries whose governments deny or restrict fundamental worker rights.

The linkage of market access with respect for worker rights has already led to the denial of trade benefits to some of the world's worst human rights and worker rights violators. More importantly perhaps, the legislation has created new opportunities for the U.S. government to join forces with the international human rights and worker rights communities to promote worker rights worldwide.

II. THE UNITED STATES' PREFERENTIAL DUTY PROGRAMS

Preferential duty programs such as the Generalized System of Preferences (GSP) and the Caribbean Basin Initiative (CBI) are designed to foster investment and economic growth in the developing world. By providing duty-free entry to designated articles from beneficiary countries, the preference programs can provide a considerable cost advantage to those products over imports from non-beneficiary countries, upon which customs duties are assessed. In order for an article from a developing country to be eligible for duty-free entry under either of the preference programs, both the product and the country of origin must be specifically designated by the President as program beneficiaries. The major factor affecting both product and country designations has traditionally been the competitive situation of the product or country involved. Under both statutory programs however, beneficiary status is now conditioned as well on the foreign government's provision of internationally recognized worker rights to workers in that country.[2]

A. The Generalized System of Preferences

Under the GSP program, the United States allows duty-free entry to approximately 3,000 designated products from 136 "beneficiary developing countries." The GSP program was established by Section 502 of the Trade Act of 1974[3] and was extended through 1993 by the Generalized System of Preferences

---

2. As we discuss below, while the GSP and CBI statutes appear to condition program benefits on an affirmative Presidential finding that the beneficiary is taking steps to afford its workers internationally recognized worker rights, in practice the Reagan Administration has shifted the burden of persuasion to those petitioners seeking to deny benefits to specific countries. In the absence of any worker rights petition concerning a particular country, the Administration will presume that such rights are being afforded to workers in that country.

3. Pub. L. No. 93-618, 88 Stat. 2066 (1975), codified at 19 U.S.C.A. § 2461 *et seq.* (1980).

Renewal Act of 1984[4] (Renewal Act). While the President has the ultimate authority to make GSP determinations, the program is administered by the Office of the United States Trade Representative (USTR) and recommendations to the President on GSP matters are made through a series of interagency committees, starting with the GSP Subcommittee of the Trade Policy Staff Committee and extending through the full Committee, then the Trade Policy Review Group, and finally the Cabinet-level Economic Policy Council.[5] Until the Renewal Act, the program imposed relatively few "social" obligations on beneficiary developing countries as a condition of receiving preferential treatment.[6]

---

4. The Renewal Act was enacted as Title V of the Trade and Tariff Act of 1984, Pub. L. No. 98-573, §§ 501-506, 98 Stat. 3020 (codified at 19 U.S.C.A. § 2461 *et seq.* [West Supp. 1988]).

5. Official announcements concerning the disposition of GSP petitions are made by the Executive Office of the President or the USTR. Regulations governing the administration of the GSP program and the decisionmaking process are issued by the USTR. *See* 15 C.F.R. §§ 2007.0-2007.8 (1987).

6. Under the 1974 Act, the President could not designate any country a "beneficiary developing country" if the country (1) were a Communist country, (2) were a member of the Organization of Petroleum Exporting Countries (OPEC), (3) afforded preferential duty treatment to the products of another country the effect of which was an adverse impact on U.S. commerce, (4) had nationalized, expropriated or otherwise seized the property of U.S. nationals, (5) did not cooperate with the United States in the control of international narcotics trafficking or (6) failed to act in good faith in recognizing or enforcing arbitral awards in favor of U.S. citizens. 19 U.S.C.A. § 2462(b)(1)-(6) (1980). A 1976 amendment to the GSP statute added the requirement that the President could not designate any country "if such country aids or abets, by granting sanctuary from prosecution to, any individual or group which has committed an act of international terrorism." 19 U.S.C.A. § 2462(b)(7) (1980).

1. The GSP's Worker Rights Provision

In the 1984 Renewal Act, Congress created several new conditions on GSP eligibility, one of which was that no country may be designated by the President as a GSP beneficiary:

> if such country has not taken or is not taking steps to afford internationally recognized worker rights to workers in the country (including any designated zone in that country).[7]

The President must also take worker rights practices into account when determining the "competitive need limits" for the products of a beneficiary country.[8]

Section 503 of the Renewal Act defines "internationally recognized worker rights" as including:

(A) the right of association;
(B) the right to organize and bargain collectively;

---

7. Trade Act of 1974, § 502(b)(7), as amended, 19 U.S.C.A. § 2462(b)(7). Other factors the President must take into account in determining whether to designate individual countries include: (1) the extent to which the country provides United States products reasonable access to its markets, 19 U.S.C.A. § 2462(c)(4); (2) the adequacy of the country's protection of U.S. intellectual property rights, 19 U.S.C.A. § 2462(c)(5); and (3) the extent to which the country has taken action to reduce trade distorting investment practices and to reduce or eliminate barriers to trade in services, 19 U.S.C.A. § 2462(c)(6).

8. 19 U.S.C.A. §§ 2464(c)(1)-(2). Under the GSP program, a "competitive need limit" (CNL) is a form of tariff-rate quota imposed on entries of particular articles from each beneficiary country. The CNL consists of two elements: a percentage limitation and an absolute value limitation. If the total entries of a given article from a particular country exceed either (1) a specified percentage of imports of that article from all countries or (2) a specified dollar value, the article will normally be "graduated" (removed) from the program at the conclusion of the subsequent Annual Review.

(C) a prohibition on the use of any form of forced or compulsory labor;
(D) a minimum age for the employment of children; and
(E) acceptable conditions of work with respect to minimum wages, hours of work, and occupational safety and health.[9]

The legislative history accompanying the Renewal Act highlighted the importance of the new worker rights provision. In the House Ways and Means Committee Report, the authors of the Renewal Act noted that:

> The Committee believes that promoting respect for the internationally recognized rights of workers is an important means of ensuring that the broadest sectors of the population within [beneficiary developing countries] benefit from the GSP program. The capacity to form unions and to bargain collectively to achieve higher wages and better working conditions is essential for workers in developing countries to attain decent living standards and to overcome hunger and poverty. The denial of internationally recognized worker rights in developing countries tend[s] to perpetuate poverty, to limit the benefits of economic development and growth, to narrow privileged elites, and to sow the seeds of social instability and political rebellion.[10]

The Committee therefore found it "appropriate" that GSP benefits be extended commensurate with the beneficiary country's respect for worker rights.[11]

At present, the statute does not detail what sorts of "steps" taken by governments to accord the enumerated worker rights would be sufficient to retain GSP eligibility. Some guidance

---

9. Trade Act of 1974, Section 502(a)(4), as amended, 19 U.S.C.A. § 2462(4).

10. H.R. Rep. No. 1090, 98th Cong., 2d Sess. 11-12, *reprinted in* 1984 U.S. Code Cong. & Ad. News 5101, 5111.

11. *Id.* at 5112.

may be offered however, in the legislative history accompanying the Overseas Private Investment Corporation (OPIC) Amendment Act of 1985.[12] OPIC is a federally chartered corporate agency of the U.S. government whose purpose is to foster development in the Third World by providing insurance and financing to private investors at favorable rates. The OPIC Amendment Act restricts OPIC's participation to projects in countries whose governments are "taking steps to adopt and implement laws that extend internationally recognized worker rights . . . to workers in that country . . . ."[13] The OPIC statute defines worker rights merely by reference to the definition in the GSP Renewal Act.[14] The House Foreign Affairs Committee Report which accompanied the 1985 OPIC amendments however, elaborated on what Congress felt were adequate steps toward extending internationally recognized worker rights:

> While there is no explicit interpretation of "taking steps to," it is the intent of the committee that a country should be considered to be "taking steps to adopt and implement laws that extend internationally recognized workers [sic] rights" if:
>
> (1) it is a member of the International Labor Organization (ILO) and a signatory of the [ILO] Constitution;
>
> (2) its laws in fact conform to one or more of the rights listed in section 502(a)(4) of the Trade Act of 1974; and
>
> (3) it continues to make progress to implement internationally recognized worker rights.[15]

---

12. Pub. L. No. 99-204, 99 Stat. 1670 (1985), codified at 22 U.S.C.A. § 2191 *et seq.* (West Supp. 1988).

13. 22 U.S.C.A. § 2191a(a)(1).

14. *Id.*

15. H.R. REP. NO. 285, 99th Cong., 1st Sess. 6, *reprinted in* 1985 U.S. CODE CONG. & AD. NEWS 2572, 2577.

The report later adds that any "progress" toward the adoption and implementation of internationally recognized worker rights must be "*visible*" in order to satisfy the third element of the "taking steps" definition in the OPIC statute.[16]

While the linkage of U.S. market access with acceptable worker rights practices is a contentious issue between the U.S. and many of its trading partners,[17] the worker rights provision of the GSP statute appears consistent with U.S. obligations under the General Agreement on Tariffs and Trade (GATT).[18] Article 18 of GATT authorizes the signatories to provide preferential duty treatment for products of developing countries and allows each signatory to frame its own conditions for participation in the program.[19] To date, only one beneficiary

---

16. *Id.* at 2576-77.

17. Most foreign governments view the provision of worker rights to be an issue strictly of domestic concern, and many of these governments feel that the United States is unlawfully encroaching upon their sovereignty by conditioning trade preferences on their domestic labor practices. While these arguments raise legitimate diplomatic issues, such issues are beyond the scope of this memorandum.

18. *Opened for Signature* Oct. 30, 1947, 61 Stat. pts. 5-6, T.I.A.S. No. 1700, 55 U.N.T.S. 194 [hereinafter GATT]. The current version of GATT is contained in GENERAL AGREEMENT ON TARIFFS AND TRADE, BASIC INSTRUMENTS AND SELECTED DOCUMENTS (Supps. I-XXXIII).

19. Waivers, Generalized System of Preferences (decision of 25 June 1971) (L/3545), GENERAL AGREEMENT ON TARIFFS AND TRADE, BASIC INSTRUMENTS AND SELECTED DOCUMENTS 24 (Supp. XVIII 1972). GATT granted a ten-year waiver of the most-favored-nation (MFN) principle of Article I of GATT in 1971 to allow fully industrialized nations to provide duty-free treatment to articles produced in developing countries so long as the scheme is "generalized, non-reciprocal and non-discriminatory." *Id.* at 25. Congress approved the Framework Agreement adopted in the Tokyo Round of (continued...)

country has challenged the application of the United States' GSP worker rights provision at the GATT.[20]

2. Administration of the Worker Rights Provision

The Renewal Act authorizes the President to enforce the worker rights provision in any of three ways: (1) through periodic "General Reviews" of country and product eligibility, (2) through Annual Reviews of country and product eligibility, or (3) at any time in which the President determines that a beneficiary country is failing to take adequate steps toward the provision of internationally recognized worker rights.

---

19. (...continued)
Multilateral Trade Negotiations which extended the GATT waiver of the MFN principle indefinitely to account for the GSP. Trade Agreements Act of 1979, Pub. L. No. 96-39 § 2(c)(11), 93 Stat. 144, 148 (1979).

See Senate Workers' Rights Hearing, *supra* note 1, at 61 (statement of Ambassador Michael B. Smith, Deputy U.S. Trade Representative) [hereinafter Smith Statement] ("[The GSP] consists of concessions unilaterally granted by the United States. Thus, the U.S. has the right not only to determine the conditions of access to the program, but also to set conditions of access which are subjective and not necessarily based on international consensus.") *See also* Note, *GSP: A System of Preferences, Not a Bargaining Lever*, 17 L. POL'Y INT'L BUS. 879, 881 at nn. 14, 15 (1985).

20. According to the State Department's representative to the GSP Subcommittee, Chile has filed a formal protest at the GATT against its suspension from the GSP program. The government of Chile has requested a review of the United States' action under the dispute consultation provisions of Article 22 of GATT and that the matter be placed before the GATT council. This document however, is not publicly available due to GATT rules of confidentiality. Interview with Mr. Joe Sala, Economic Officer of the Office of Developing Countries, U.S. Department of State (State Department Representative to the Trade Policy Staff Committee's GSP Subcommittee) (July 27, 1988) [hereinafter Sala Interview].

Section 505(b) of the GSP Renewal Act[21] requires the President to conduct periodic General Reviews of country and product eligibility on the basis of the revised eligibility criteria of the Act, which include protection of worker rights. The first General Review to follow the Renewal Act was conducted by the GSP Subcommittee during 1985 and 1986;[22] its results were published on January 6, 1987.[23] As a result of the Trade Policy Staff Committee's recommendations following the Review, the President determined to remove Nicaragua and Romania from the GSP program altogether and to suspend Paraguay's eligibility. The review of Chile's worker rights practices was extended for an additional year and Chile was eventually suspended from the program in December 1987.[24] The President determined that the governments of Guatemala, Haiti, the Philippines, South Korea, Suriname, Taiwan and Zaire had taken or were taking sufficient steps to accord internationally recognized worker rights to workers in those countries and would therefore remain eligible for GSP benefits. The GSP Subcommittee does not anticipate another General Review of the GSP program unless the program is extended beyond 1993.[25]

The GSP Subcommittee also conducts Annual Reviews to determine both country and product eligibility for GSP benefits.[26] The first Annual Review to follow the Renewal

---

21. Codified at 19 U.S.C.A. § 2464(c)(2)(A).

22. This proceeding included reviews of worker rights practices in Chile, Guatemala, Haiti, Nicaragua, South Korea, Paraguay, the Philippines, Romania, Suriname, Taiwan, and Zaire. Memorandum of January 2, 1987: Actions Concerning the Generalized System of Preferences, 52 Fed. Reg. 389 (1987)

23. *Id.*

24. Proclamation No. 5758, 52 Fed. Reg. 49,129 (1987).

25. Any further review of worker rights practices will take place within the content of the Annual Review process, discussed *infra*. Sala Interview, *supra* note 20.

26. The annual reviews are conducted pursuant to USTR regulations codified at 15 C.F.R. § 2007.3 (1987).

Act was conducted by the Subcommittee in 1987; its results were issued in April 1988.[27] In its press release, the USTR announced the President's determination to retain the GSP beneficiary status of Taiwan, Korea, Indonesia, Thailand and Turkey due to improvements in the labor practices of their governments. The agency announced that the review of one beneficiary, the Central African Republic, would continue for an additional year.[28] The 1988 Annual Review is pending.[29]

The GSP Subcommittee has never conducted an investigation of worker rights practices outside the context of a General or Annual Review, although the statute gives the President the authority to do so if he finds it appropriate.[30]

---

27. U.S. TRADE REPRESENTATIVE, ANNUAL REVIEW OF THE GENERALIZED SYSTEM OF PREFERENCES (GSP) WORKER RIGHTS 1 (April 1, 1988) (available from the Office of the U.S. Trade Representative, GSP Subcommittee) [hereinafter USTR 1987 GSP ANNUAL REVIEW]. During this review, the Trade Policy Staff Committee agreed to consider worker rights petitions filed against the governments of the Central African Republic, Indonesia, South Korea, Taiwan and Turkey, but refused to review petitions filed against El Salvador, Guatemala, Haiti, Singapore, Suriname and Zambia. These determinations are discussed *infra.*

28. *Id.* at 12.

29. On August 25, 1988, the USTR announced the Trade Policy Staff Committee's determination to review the worker rights practices of Burma, Haiti, Israel, Liberia, Malaysia and Syria following the submission of worker rights petitions seeking the termination of GSP benefits to those countries. The Committee has also determined to reject worker rights petition concerning El Salvador, Guatemala, Indonesia, the Philippines, Thailand and Turkey. U.S. Trade Representative, Yeutter Accepts Worker Rights Petitions for GSP Review 2 (August 25, 1988) (available from the Office of the U.S. Trade Representative). *See also* Generalized System of Preferences (GSP); Review of Country Practice Petitions and Public Hearings, 53 Fed. Reg. 33,208 (1988).

30. 19 U.S.C.A. § 2464(a); *see also* 15 C.F.R. § 2007.0(f).

a. Petitioning the Trade Policy Staff Committee on Worker Rights Violations During the GSP Annual Review

The GSP statute requires the Trade Policy Staff Committee to take worker rights practices into account during its Annual Review to determine the country- and product-eligibility of particular countries to participate in the GSP program. As discussed below[31] however, the Committee normally does not review a country's worker rights practices unless a petitioner comes forward during the Annual Review to challenge the provision of worker rights in that country. The USTR's requirement of standing to petition the Committee to review a beneficiary country's worker rights practices varies with the type of remedy sought by the petitioner.

Under the GSP regulation, "*any person*" may petition the Committee to review the country-eligibility status of any beneficiary designated country with respect to the designation criteria listed in Section 502(c) of the GSP statute, which include the worker rights provision.[32] A petition seeking a product-eligibility review[33] however, may only be brought by

---

31. *See infra* text at 21-22.

32. 15 C.F.R. § 2007.0(b).

33. A review of "product" eligibility focuses on the "competitiveness" of the article for purposes of establishing or modifying the competitive need limits for such articles. While a product eligibility review normally entails an investigation of a country's ability to produce the article at a cost that is competitive with other world producers, the Committee must also review the designation criteria (including the provision of worker rights) in making its determination of an article's competitiveness. 19 U.S.C.A. § 2464(c)(2)(A); 15 C.F.R. § 2007.8(b)(2)(x).

The Committee has previously used other country-eligibility criteria from the Renewal Act in reducing the competitive need limits for particular beneficiaries. (continued...)

an "interested party"[34] defined as "a party who has significant economic interest in the subject matter of the request, or any other party that would be materially affected by the action requested."[35] This regulatory language would appear to preclude a human rights organization from bringing a product-eligibility petition unless that organization brought its case in conjunction with a labor union or another organization representing U.S. workers or industries. Once a product-eligibility review is initiated by an interested party however, the regulation permits "any other person" to intervene in the proceeding and make submissions concerning the substantive elements of the review.[36]

The agency's timetable regarding the submission and adjudication of country-practice petitions and product-eligibility petitions during the Annual Review is set out at 15 C.F.R. Section 2007.3. The regulation also specifies informational requirements for country-practice petitions[37] and product-eligibility petitions.[38]

b. The Annual Review Process

The Annual Review process is an interagency proceeding conducted by the GSP Subcommittee of the Trade Policy Staff Committee which then makes recommendations to the full Committee. The Subcommittee is made up of representatives

---

33. (...continued)
Following the General Review of 1985-1986, it announced that it would reduce the CNLs on 34 categories of Mexican products in retaliation for Mexico's failure to provide adequate protection for U.S. intellectual property rights, particularly with regard to U.S. pharmaceutical patents. Memorandum of January 2, 1987: Actions Concerning the Generalized System of Preferences, 52 Fed. Reg. 389 (1987).

34. 15 C.F.R. § 2007.0(a).

35. 15 C.F.R. § 2007.0(d).

36. 15 C.F.R. § 2007.0(c).

37. 15 C.F.R. § 2007.0(b).

38. 15 C.F.R. § 2007.1(a).

from the Departments of State, Labor, Commerce, Agriculture and Treasury. The Subcommittee adjudicates worker rights petitions in two phases during the Annual Review. Phase One begins on June 1 of each year, the deadline for submission of all GSP petitions concerning country practices.[39] In each case, this phase involves a preliminary determination as to whether the petition meets the regulatory standards for review.

Under the USTR's regulation, the Trade Policy Staff Committee must accept any petition concerning worker rights unless one of the following factors is present: (1) the petition fails to satisfy the informational requirements of 15 C.F.R. § 2007.0(b) or fails to state a worker rights violation within the meaning of the Renewal Act[40] or (2) the country's practices have been the subject of a previous worker rights review and the petition fails to present "substantial new information warranting further consideration of the issue."[41] In practice however, the Committee has created a third basis for rejecting worker rights petitions during Phase One. Under this rule, the petition will be rejected if the Committee or another agency of the federal government has sufficient evidence on hand to rebut the factual basis of each allegation put forth by the petitioner concerning the beneficiary country.[42]

On July 15, the Committee concludes Phase One by announcing in the *Federal Register* which of the petitions the agency received it has accepted for review.

If the Committee accepts the petition for review, the agency initiates Phase Two of the review process. During this

---

39. 15 C.F.R. § 2007.3(a)(1).

40. 15 C.F.R. § 2007.2(2).

41. 15 C.F.R. § 2007.0(b).

42. A worker rights petition filed against the government of El Salvador was rejected for review by the Committee on this basis during the General Review of 1985-1986. Interview with Mr. Hiram Lawrence, Chairman, GSP Subcommittee, Office of the U.S. Trade Representative (July 22, 1988) [hereinafter Lawrence Interview].

stage of the proceeding, the GSP Subcommittee collects information concerning the country's worker rights practices and makes a recommendation to the full Committee concerning the merits of the petition. In gathering the necessary information, the GSP Subcommittee consults with the labor attaché at the American Embassy or Consulate in the country at issue. The attaché then gathers information relevant to the proceeding from both government and non-government sources. The Subcommittee also receives information from the regional labor expert at the Department of Labor in Washington. The Subcommittee does not send representatives to the country to investigate labor conditions first-hand, apparently due to investigative resource limitations.[43]

While the Committee frequently discusses the worker rights petition with the government of the beneficiary country involved, it is neither the policy nor practice of the agency to attempt to "negotiate" improved worker rights practices with the government under review.[44] During the pendency of these investigations, the GSP Subcommittee holds public hearings to give interested parties an opportunity to comment on the investigation and to rebut evidence presented by the opposing parties.[45]

When all of the relevant factual information is collected, the GSP Subcommittee makes a recommendation to the full Trade Policy Staff Committee. If the latter is unable to reach a consensus concerning an individual petition, the case is decided by majority vote. The dissenting agency may then appeal to the Trade Policy Review Group, which is composed of executive department representatives at the under secretary

---

43. The agency also believes the labor attachés to be adequate in performing this function. Conversation with Mr. Tom White, Office of Developing Countries, U.S. Department of State (August 3, 1988).

44. Lawrence Interview, *supra* note 42. However, the Committee has taken proposed labor reforms in a beneficiary country into account when making recommendations to the President.

45. 15 C.F.R. §§ 2007.2(d), 2003(a)(3).

level. If the dissenting agency is dissatisfied with the Group's disposition of the matter, the case is referred to the Economic Policy Council, composed of Cabinet members, which reviews the matter and makes a final recommendation to the President concerning the petition.[46]

c. Substantive Standards Governing the Consideration of Worker Rights Petitions

The GSP statute currently offers no guidance as to what factors the Trade Policy Staff Committee must consider in reviewing worker rights petitions or as to the standards or the burden of persuasion to be applied in these proceedings. Moreover, the USTR has yet to promulgate substantive standards governing the consideration of worker rights petitions brought against GSP beneficiary countries although many on the Committee recognize the need to clarify the rules governing such proceedings.[47] Such matters are apparently determined on a case-by-case basis at the Committee's discretion.

The standards applied by the Committee in making previous recommendations to the President concerning worker rights petitions remain somewhat unclear following the General Review of 1985-1986 and the Annual Review of 1987. This is due primarily to the relative secrecy and informality of the process in which such determinations are made. While the agency does hold public hearings during the Annual Review process to afford interested parties an opportunity to comment, the actual determinations concerning the petitions are not conducted pursuant to the Administrative Procedure Act[48] nor are the President's final decisions subject to judicial review.[49] Finally, nearly all of the factual information collected by the

---

46. 15 C.F.R. § 2007.2(g). Lawrence Interview, *supra* note 42.

47. Lawrence Interview, *supra* note 42; Sala Interview, *supra* note 20.

48. 5 U.S.C.A. § 551 *et seq.* (1977).

49. *See* Florsheim Shoe Co. v. United States, 744 F.2d 787, 795 (Fed. Cir. 1984) (President's findings of fact and motivations for his actions under GSP program are not subject to review).

Committee during the course of its investigation is never made available for public inspection.[50]

(1) Standards Applied in Phase One Determinations

According to the USTR's regulation, the Trade Policy Staff Committee should not apply any substantive criteria in its recommendation to the President concerning the acceptance or rejection of a worker rights petition for review. Instead, the Committee should recommend rejection only if the petition is facially deficient in some form or if the subject country's worker rights practices have been previously reviewed by the Committee and found acceptable by the President. A considerable amount of public and Congressional criticism has been directed at the President's previous Phase One determinations however, particularly in cases where the USTR has declined to specify in sufficient detail the factual basis or legal reasoning behind the President's decision.[51]

During Phase One of the 1987 Annual Review, the President rejected worker rights petitions concerning El Salvador, Guatemala, Haiti, Singapore, Suriname and Zambia. The USTR claimed that the worker rights practices of Guatemala, Haiti and Suriname had been sufficiently reviewed during the General Review of 1985-1986 and that the 1987 petitions contained no substantially new information to merit review. The agency offered no public explanation however, for the President's rejection of the petitions concerning El Salvador, Singapore and Zambia. The rejection of the El Salvador

50. This practice appears due in part to the need to prevent reprisals against individuals within the beneficiary countries who cooperate with the U.S. government during the review process.

51. Sala Interview, *supra* note 20. The USTR does not publish any explanatory opinions concerning its Phase One determinations in the *Federal Register*. Under the USTR regulation however, the agency is required to provide the worker rights petitioner with a written explanation of the action taken on the petition, including a negative Phase One determination. 15 C.F.R. § 2007.2(2).

petition generated considerable protest from the United States human rights community including some Members of Congress.[52] Many persons who supported the petition charged that the President's rejection was politically motivated and demanded an official explanation from the USTR. The agency has since explained that the U.S. Embassy in El Salvador provided the Committee with evidence refuting each of the petitioners' specific allegations concerning worker rights violations.[53]

At present, the extent to which political considerations and other factors unrelated to the sufficiency of individual petitions play a role in the President's Phase One determinations is unclear. One member of the GSP Subcommittee however, has pointed out the rationale behind having some degree of executive discretion in making Phase One determinations. To many officials involved in the GSP review process, the Annual Review has recently become attractive to a certain type of "worker rights" petitioner who seeks a public forum (available in Phase Two) to lambast foreign countries for reasons unrelated to worker rights practices.[54] These officials fear that if such petitioners were allowed to proceed to Phase Two, the public hearing would become a media "circus" in which the discussion of worker rights would be drowned out by unrelated and irrelevant allegations. Therefore, the argument follows, it is necessary for the President to reject certain ill-founded or bad faith "worker rights" petitions in order to preserve the integrity of the review process.

(2) Standards Applied in Phase Two Determinations

As in the case of Phase One determinations, it is difficult to identify any comprehensive set of criteria that the Trade Policy Staff Committee applies in Phase Two of the review process to recommend to the President whether a beneficiary

---

52. Letter from Rep. Donald J. Pease to Clayton Yeutter, U.S. Trade Representative (August 18, 1987).

53. Lawrence Interview, *supra* note 42.

54. Sala Interview, *supra* note 20.

country's government is taking adequate steps toward affording worker rights in that country. The USTR does not publish extensive opinions regarding the disposition of individual worker rights petitions although it does distribute rather terse and conclusory press releases at the end of its worker rights investigations. Interviews with key officials involved in such determinations, as well as a review of the agency's press releases following the General Review of 1985-1986 (completed in January 1987) and the 1987 Annual Review (completed in April 1988), do shed some light as to what factors the Committee considers relevant in its review of worker rights practices.

The Committee appears to give the greatest weight to legal provisions in the beneficiary countries that bear upon the five categories of internationally recognized worker rights as enumerated in the GSP statute.[55] The agency focuses on laws pertaining to the right to form independent labor organizations and to bargain collectively as well as the right to strike. The agency often reviews laws that place conditions, formalities and other restrictions on these rights. The Committee also reviews laws and regulations pertaining to the employment of children in the subject country. Where applicable, the agency investigates allegations that the government permits forced or compulsory labor.[56]

In countries where industrial unions are legally permitted, the agency attempts to determine whether these organizations are legitimately representative of workers in that industry or whether they are dominated by the government. This determination usually turns on an evaluation of legal provisions relating to the election or appointment of union officials. The agency also examines the extent to which collective bargaining is allowed beyond the enterprise level and whether indigenous

---

55. *See supra* text accompanying note 9.

56. U.S. TRADE REPRESENTATIVE, GENERAL REVIEW OF THE GENERALIZED SYSTEM OF PREFERENCES (GSP), WORKER RIGHTS 6 (1987) (discussing Haitian labor practices) (available from the Office of the U.S. Trade Representative, GSP Subcommittee of the Trade Policy Staff Committee) [hereinafter USTR GSP GENERAL REVIEW].

local or national labor organizations are permitted to establish ties with and receive material and technical support from international labor organizations.[57]

In many instances, a beneficiary country's government will prohibit public sector employees from striking or from organizing independent labor unions. In some of these cases, the Committee has considered whether the government provides alternative methods of dispute resolution to public employees, such as grievance procedures.[58]

The Committee appears to assign only moderate significance to provisions concerning minimum wages, maximum hours and occupational safety and health standards since such provisions represent the most quantitative of the enumerated worker rights in the GSP statute and must be viewed within the context of the country's level of economic development.[59] Where a country's laws do contain explicit guarantees of minimum wages, maximum hours and the like, the Committee has documented, to the extent possible, the level of enforcement of these provisions, including the number of prosecutions brought against employers suspected of violating the provisions.[60]

Generally, the agency appears to accept legal provisions or executive pronouncements that grant worker rights at face value and in most cases has not delved deeply into a country's administration and enforcement of such provisions to determine if the rights granted thereby actually exist in practice. In one instance however, the agency did review the actual provision of worker rights and determined that despite official pronouncements to the contrary, the government of the

57. USTR 1987 GSP ANNUAL REVIEW, *supra* note 27, at 11 (discussing Turkish labor practices).

58. *Id.* at 9 (discussing Indonesian labor practices).

59. *Id.* at 1.

60. *Id.* at 5 (discussing Taiwanese labor practices).

beneficiary country "failed to comply with both the spirit and letter of these assurances" as a matter of practice.[61]

By far the most problematic factor the agency has encountered in administering worker rights petitions is a petitioner's allegation of specific incidents of abduction, torture and murder of union members or officials at the hands of government agents of the beneficiary country. As GSP Subcommittee officials are quick to point out, the agency has experienced considerable difficulty in distinguishing violations of "worker rights,"[62] which are grounds for GSP termination under the statute, from violations of "human rights"[63] which,

---

61. USTR GSP GENERAL REVIEW, *supra* note 56, at 5 (discussing Paraguayan labor practices: noting the government's "repression of new union-organizing efforts and a wave of labor-related arrests" during the investigation). While it is evident from the above language that the Committee conducted a relatively extensive review of the Paraguay's labor practices, it is nonetheless unclear from the USTR's publicly-distributed decision what actual factors led the agency to advise the President that the Paraguayan government was not taking adequate steps to provide internationally recognized worker rights to its citizens.

62. *See supra* text accompanying note 9.

63. While definitions of "human rights" vary, Section 116(a) of the Foreign Assistance Act of 1961, as amended, defines the violation of "internationally recognized human rights" as "torture or cruel, inhuman, or degrading treatment or punishment, prolonged detention without charges, causing the disappearance of persons by the abduction and clandestine detention of those persons, or other flagrant denial of the right to life, liberty, and the security of person." 22 U.S.C.A. § 2151n(a) (West Supp. 1988).

The State Department extends this definition in its annual human rights report to the Congress: ". . . [our] reports unashamedly reflect the U.S. view that the right of self-government is a basic political right, that government is legitimate only when grounded on the consent of the governed,

(continued...)

standing alone, are not a basis for such termination.[64] In cases where a petitioner has relied heavily on such individual occurrences as the basis for seeking the country's removal from the GSP, the Committee has attempted to determine whether the victims listed in the petition were targeted by the country's government as part of systematic endeavor to deny worker rights or whether the individuals were singled out for political activities unrelated to worker rights. As a result of the difficulty in drawing such distinctions, the agency does not appear to give substantial weight to isolated incidents involving individual victims, but instead appears to look for a pattern of government action that evinces a clear intent to deny its workers one or more of the five categories of worker rights as defined by the Renewal Act.[65]

(3) Factors Supporting the President's Termination of GSP Benefits to Nicaragua, Paraguay, Romania and Chile

Only four beneficiary developing countries have lost their GSP designation as a result of worker rights practices since the Renewal Act was passed in 1984: Chile, Nicaragua, Paraguay and Romania. Issues involved in the review of Chile's labor

---

63. (...continued)
and that government thus grounded should not be used to deny life, liberty, and the pursuit of happiness. Individuals in a society have the inalienable right to be free from governmental violations of the integrity of the person; to enjoy civil liberties such as freedom of expression, assembly, religion, and movement, without discrimination based on race, ancestry, or sex; and to change their government by peaceful means." STATE DEP'T REPORT TO HOUSE COMM. ON FOREIGN AFFAIRS & SENATE COMM. ON FOREIGN RELATIONS, 100TH CONG., 2D SESS., COUNTRY REPORTS ON HUMAN RIGHTS PRACTICES FOR 1987 3 (Joint Comm. Print 1988) [hereinafter 1987 STATE DEP'T COUNTRY REPORTS].

64. Lawrence Interview, *supra* note 42.

65. USTR GSP GENERAL REVIEW, *supra* note 56, at 6 (discussing Surinamese labor practices).

practices included freedom of association and the right to organize and bargain collectively. The petitioners in this case alleged that collective bargaining in Chile was limited to the level of individual firms; that the government restricted the establishment of large cross-sectoral national labor confederations; that political freedom for trade unions was restricted; and that Chile had committed severe acts of harassment and violence against independent trade union leaders and members.[66]

The Trade Policy Staff Committee found upon review that the Chilaen government had taken some measures to reduce restrictions on labor unions including: reducing the number of industrial categories where strikes were not permitted; establishing special labor courts; providing assurances that the government would not condone the harassment of unions or labor leaders; eliminating certain financial reporting requirements and limiting the use of audits for harassment purposes. Based on these assurances, the Committee agreed to extend the review for an additional year. Upon further review however, the President eventually determined that Chile had not followed through on its promises to improve protection of worker rights and suspended its participation in the GSP program, effective February 29, 1988.[67]

Following its investigation of Nicaragua, the USTR announced that

> Our review of Nicaragua's worker rights practices found that the Government of Nicaragua is not taking steps to afford its workers internationally recognized workers rights. In particular, we found that freedom of association has been suspended in Nicaragua and that the Government of Nicaragua has sharply limited the rights of unions to organize and bargain.[68]

---

66. *Id.* at 2.

67. Proclamation No. 5758, 52 Fed. Reg. 49,129 (1987).

68. USTR GSP GENERAL REVIEW, *supra* note 56, at 5.

The President removed Nicaragua from the GSP program effective March 4, 1987.

In the case of Paraguay, the Committee's review found "substantial government restrictions on, or interference with, freedom of association and the right to organize and bargain collectively."[69] Despite commitments from the Paraguayan government in 1986 to ease restrictions on union activity, the Committee found continuing violations in "the repression of new union-organizing efforts and a wave of labor-related arrests in late 1986."[70] The President suspended Paraguay from the GSP program effective March 4, 1987.

The Committee's review of Romanian worker rights practices concluded that "steps were not being taken by the Government of Romania to afford its workers internationally recognized worker rights. We found that two of the fundamental categories of worker rights, freedom of association and the right to organize and bargain collectively, do not exist in Romania."[71] The President removed Romania from the GSP program effective March 4, 1987.

d. The Burden of Persuasion Imposed In Review Proceedings

As a matter of administrative practice, it would appear that the Trade Policy Staff Committee under the Reagan Administration places the burden of proof with regard to worker rights violations upon the petitioner rather than on the beneficiary government under review. Moreover, in the absence of a worker rights petition concerning a particular country, the Committee appears to presume that the government affords internationally recognized worker rights to its workers and will not subject the country to any worker rights review whatsoever.

---

69. *Id.*

70. *Id.*

71. *Id.* at 6.

e. Conclusion

Without more detailed decisions from the Trade Policy Staff Committee concerning worker rights petitions, it is virtually impossible to identify or predict with any certainty the standards the agency will use in future worker rights determinations. One tendency is clear, however. The agency has been far more likely to find a denial of worker rights in particular beneficiary countries when it has looked beyond mere legislation or governmental pronouncements concerning worker rights and has gathered reliable non-governmental documentation of labor practices within the country. This healthful mistrust of official pronouncements was evident in the Committee's investigations of Chile, Nicaragua, Paraguay and Romania, discussed above. In many instances where the Committee found acceptable worker rights practices, it appeared to accept the official governmental labor policy as reality and refrained from conducting a searching probe of labor conditions. To be sure, all such determinations are influenced in part by foreign policy concerns, investigative resource limitations and access barriers imposed by the beneficiary countries themselves. Whether these considerations may have led the agency to disregard or minimize legitimate claims of worker rights violations in review proceedings concerning countries such as El Salvador or Haiti is unclear.

B. The Caribbean Basin Initiative

The Caribbean Basin Initiative (CBI) program, enacted in 1983,[72] allows duty-free entry to certain articles from designated beneficiary countries in the Caribbean and Central America. Eligibility for preferential treatment under the CBI is based on an executive determination that the country meets seven mandatory and eleven discretionary criteria. One of the discretionary criteria which the President must take into account in designating a country as eligible for CBI is "the degree to which workers in such country are afforded reasonable workplace conditions and enjoy the right to organize and

---

72. Pub. L. No. 98-67, 97 Stat. 384 (1983), codified at 19 U.S.C.A. § 2701 *et seq.* (West Supp. 1988).

bargain collectively."[73] All of these criteria were considered by the President in making initial designations of CBI eligibility in 1984.

The CBI differs from the GSP in that it does not provide for periodic review of a beneficiary's labor practices once the initial determination is made by the President that the government accords the enumerated worker rights to laborers within that country. Further, the CBI statute does not provide for interested parties to petition the Trade Policy Staff Committee to review individual cases of worker rights violations. Thus, the initial designation of a CBI beneficiary lasts for the duration of the twelve-year preference program.[74]

According to the USTR, permanent CBI designation is designed to encourage foreign investors to locate their operations in the designated CBI beneficiaries.[75] Under the permanent designation scheme, the CBI program offers a more reliable guarantee of preferential duty treatment than that currently offered by the GSP program, which is subject to periodic review concerning, *inter alia*, the worker rights practices of the beneficiary country's government.

To date, no country otherwise eligible for CBI designation has been denied benefits under the program due to worker rights violations. However, at the outset of the CBI program when the Trade Policy Staff Committee was formulating its initial recommendations for designation to the President, the governments of Haiti, the Dominican Republic, Honduras and

---

73. 19 U.S.C.A. § 2702(c)(8).

74. The program is scheduled to expire on September 30, 1995. 19 U.S.C.A. § 2706.

75. Telephone conversation with Mr. John Rosenbaum, Office of the U.S. Trade Representative (July 20, 1988) [hereinafter Rosenbaum Interview].

El Salvador pledged to improve labor conditions in their countries.[76]

Four CBI-eligible countries, El Salvador, Guatemala, Haiti and Nicaragua, have been the subject of worker rights petitions under the GSP program. One of them, Nicaragua, was terminated from the GSP program due to worker rights violations.[77] Under Reagan Administrative practice however, the worker rights investigations under the GSP program would not have altered the beneficiary status of the same countries under the CBI since the programs are administered independently of one another.[78] Moreover, some critics have charged that the Reagan Administration's enforcement of the worker rights provision in the CBI statute has been "non-existent".[79]

C. The Efficacy of Using Preferential Duty Programs as Leverage to Promote Worker Rights Abroad

An analysis of the efficacy of using preferential duty programs to promote worker rights abroad involves an assessment of the risks presented by such programs as well as their actual effectiveness in promoting worker rights.

The conditioning of preferential duty benefits on respect for worker rights is certainly the least confrontational method of using import trade regulation as a vehicle to promote respect for such rights abroad. Because the benefits extended by the United States under the GSP and CBI programs are unilateral and are not required by any multilateral trade agreement, the anti-discrimination provisions of GATT do not appear to

---

76. *Id.* *See also* INTERNATIONAL LABOR RIGHTS EDUCATION AND RESEARCH FUND, TRADE'S HIDDEN COSTS: WORKER RIGHTS IN A CHANGING WORLD ECONOMY 49 (1988) [hereinafter TRADE'S HIDDEN COSTS].

77. *See supra* text accompanying note 68.

78. Rosenbaum Interview, *supra* note 75.

79. TRADE'S HIDDEN COSTS, *supra* note 76, at 49.

apply.[80] The United States is therefore free to attach any conditions to preferential treatment that it pleases. The worker rights conditions of the GSP and CBI programs are therefore less likely to result in diplomatic disputes with America's trading partners than are other proposals concerning the linkage of market access with respect for worker rights.[81]

The administrative experience of the GSP and CBI programs however, has highlighted some of the inherent limitations on using preferential duty programs to promote respect for worker rights in the developing world. First, the benefits can only operate to induce greater respect for worker rights on the part of those countries whose products are eligible or potentially eligible for duty-free entry under the GSP or CBI. Currently GSP designation is limited to developing countries; the statute expressly forbids GSP participation by industrialized nations including most European countries and Japan.[82] The statute also excludes members of OPEC, most of the Eastern-Bloc states and the Republic of South Africa from participation in the program.[83] Finally, the USTR recently announced that South Korea, Taiwan and Singapore, each of whom is widely considered to have committed substantial violations of worker rights in the past, will be graduated from

---

80. *See* Smith Statement, *supra* note 19, at 61 ("[The GSP] consists of concessions unilaterally granted by the United States. Thus, the U.S. has the right not only to determine the conditions of access to the program, but also to set conditions of access which are subjective and not necessarily based on international consensus").

81. *See* Parts III and IV *infra* for a discussion of Section 301 of the Trade Act of 1974 and the International Emergency Economic Powers Act.

82. 19 U.S.C.A. § 2462(b).

83. *Id.* Other exclusionary categories are listed at 19 U.S.C.A. § 2462(b)(1)-(7).

the program along with Hong Kong on January 1, 1989.[84] CBI benefits are limited to designated countries in the Caribbean and Central America. These restrictions on designation currently preclude any program-based incentive for countries such as Poland, Saudi Arabia or South Africa to improve their worker rights practices and will now preclude actions involving Taiwan, South Korea or Singapore.

Second, for many countries that are eligible or potentially eligible for preferential duty treatment, the limited benefits offered by the GSP and CBI programs may not constitute sufficient economic inducement to reverse long-standing traditions of worker rights violations. Duty-free entry under the GSP or CBI confers a comparative advantage upon designated articles over similar articles from non-beneficiary countries. This advantage is measured by the prevailing duty rate for the applicable tariff category and generally ranges around 5-7% *ad valorem* for articles of non-communist origin. If a beneficiary country's government should conclude that the denial of worker rights imparts a greater cost advantage to its exports than the benefit that accrues from GSP or CBI designation, the government could be expected to forego such designation rather than surrender the superior economic benefit arising from worker rights suppression.

This limitation is particularly apparent in cases where a beneficiary country's trade volume with the United States is so low and the corresponding aggregate GSP benefits so insignificant that the potential economic impact of termination from the program is insufficient to elicit a serious response from the country's government. The Trade Policy Staff Committee appears to be facing this problem in its pending

---

84. Proclamation No. 5805, 53 Fed. Reg. 15,785, 15,786 (1988). While South Korea, Taiwan, and Singapore had previously been the subject of public interest group petitions to revoke GSP benefits on the basis of worker rights violations, the President's decision to graduate these countries along with Hong Kong was based on a determination that the four Asian countries had reached sufficient levels of economic development so as to no longer merit preferential duty treatment under the GSP. Hong Kong has never been the subject of a worker rights petition.

review of Liberia, a country that received less than $10,000 in total GSP benefits in 1987.[85]

Other problems have also become apparent in the administration of the worker rights provisions of the GSP and CBI. The United States' promotion of human rights abroad has traditionally been the domain of the State Department which even today conducts most of the fact-finding necessary for the Committee's recommendation to the President as to whether the beneficiary country under review is taking adequate steps toward providing the GSP's enumerated worker rights within its borders.[86] The purpose of the preference programs however, is to promote economic development in the Third World. As such, these programs are an integral component of the United States' trade policy and their day-to-day administration is delegated to the President's trade policy arm, the USTR.

The USTR does not consider itself a human rights agency and has made it clear that it cannot and does not play the role of international policeman with regard to working conditions abroad.[87] As an agency devoted to the promotion and liberalization of trade between the United States and its trading partners, the USTR finds itself in an awkward position trying to encourage export-oriented investment in developing countries while at the same time participating in GSP proceedings to determine whether or not to deny preferential treatment to many of those same countries for reasons unrelated to current U.S. trade policy.[88] Nevertheless, the GSP Subcommittee

---

85. Lawrence Interview, *supra* note 42.

86. The State Department annually publishes the United States Government's comprehensive statement concerning human rights and worker rights practices throughout the world. *See* 1987 STATE DEP'T COUNTRY REPORTS, *supra* note 63.

87. Lawrence Interview, *supra* note 42.

88. Other conditions of participation imposed by the GSP Renewal Act and the CBI, such as ·respect by beneficiary countries for U.S. intellectual property rights, *are* considered by the USTR to be integral components of U.S. trade policy. *See*
(continued...)

personnel who coordinate the U.S. government's administration of worker rights petitions point out three types of beneficiary countries where a worker rights petition might produce some constructive results.

First, a country that generates a substantial level of GSP-eligible exports to the United States would have a significant economic interest in defending its practices against a worker rights petition. In recent years, a large proportion of all GSP benefits has been heavily concentrated in a small number of countries. In 1987 for example, the four "Pacific Tigers," Hong Kong, Singapore, South Korea and Taiwan, accounted for 59% of all GSP-eligible exports to the United States. For this reason, the worker rights petitions filed against Taiwan, Singapore and Korea during the General Review of 1985-1986 and the 1987 Annual Review generated considerable responses from those governments.

On April 29, 1988, the President announced his decision to "graduate" (remove) the four Tigers from the GSP program effective January 1, 1989, for reasons unrelated to worker rights practices.[89] Once these countries are removed in 1989, the program's top beneficiaries in terms of GSP-eligible trade will be Mexico, Brazil, Thailand, Israel, Malaysia and the

---

88. (...continued)
19 U.S.C.A. § 2462(c)(5) (protection of intellectual property as condition of participation in GSP program); 19 U.S.C.A. § 2702(c)(9) (protection of intellectual property as condition of participation in CBI program). These policy goals are more actively pursued by the Reagan Administration. *See, e.g.*, Unfair Trade Practices: Brazil's Lack of Adequate Intellectual Property Protection for Pharmaceuticals and Fine Chemicals (Investigation under Section 301 of the Trade Act of 1974, Notice of Public Hearings and Request for Public Comments), 53 Fed. Reg. 28,100 (1988).

89. Proclamation No. 5805, 53 Fed. Reg. 15,785, 15,786 (1988). *See* note 84 *supra*.

Philippines.[90] With the exceptions of Mexico and Brazil, each of these beneficiaries is already the subject of a worker rights petition in the pending 1988 Annual Review.[91]

Second, a country that does not generate considerable GSP-eligible exports to the United States but which nonetheless relies heavily on OPIC benefits to attract foreign investment would also have a significant economic interest in the outcome of a worker rights determination. Under current administrative practice, a determination by the Trade Policy Staff Committee that a country does not accord internationally recognized worker rights to its citizens is given preclusive effect by OPIC. Following such a determination, OPIC suspends its participation in projects within that country.[92]

Third, a country that maintains close political, diplomatic, economic or military ties with the United States or which plays a prominent role in multilateral organizations and affairs might view a worker rights petition as a significant threat to its relations with the United States or to its international reputation. Such a country would be more likely than most to take an active role in the petition review process to secure a favorable determination from the U.S. government concerning its worker rights practices.

Two review proceedings in which this third set of factors may have produced favorable results were the investigations of

---

90. U.S. TRADE REPRESENTATIVE, 1987 GSP TOP 15 BENEFICIARIES LIST (available from the Office of the U.S. Trade Representative).

91. U.S. TRADE REPRESENTATIVE, U.S. GENERALIZED SYSTEM OF PREFERENCES LISTING OF COUNTRY PRACTICE PETITIONS, 1988 ANNUAL REVIEW (available from the Office of the U.S. Trade Representative) (June 1988).

92. The suspension of OPIC benefits applies only to new projects or programs originating after the Committee's determination. OPIC will continue to honor its commitments to existing projects within the country. Conversation with Mr. Harvey Himberg, Overseas Private Investment Corporation (August 15, 1988).

Turkey and Thailand during the 1987 Annual Review. During the review, the Turkish government agreed to modify certain restrictions in its labor code concerning union activity by June 1988. The restrictions to be modified include: 1) the requirement that an employee work one year in a workplace before engaging in organizing activities; 2) the limit of four consecutive terms for union officers; 3) the prohibition of unionization of teachers and civil servants; and 4) the government approval requirement for international affiliation.[93]

The Thai government informed the Committee during the 1987 Annual Review that it planned to seek parliamentary passage in 1988 of a new "Labor Protection Law" which would grant increased protection for Thai children who were at risk of being contracted out to industrial employers by their parents. The proposed legislation would raise the minimum working age in Thailand for most occupations from twelve to thirteen; increase the authority of the Thai Department of Labor inspectors; abolish oral labor contracts; and prohibit the advance payment of wages to parties other than the employed children. The Thai government also pledged to assist children in overcoming economic barriers to remaining in school by providing funds for uniforms, meals and transportation.[94]

It is still too early to conclude that the assurances made by the Turkish and Thai governments will lead to measurable improvements in the respect for worker rights in those countries. Nonetheless, the very fact that some governments of beneficiary countries have responded constructively to worker rights reviews is grounds for modest confidence in the potential ability of the U.S. government to promote respect for these rights by conditioning participation in preferential duty programs.

---

93. USTR 1987 GSP ANNUAL REVIEW, *supra* note 27, at 10-11 (discussing Turkish labor practices).

94. *Id.* at 7 (discussing Thai labor practices).

D. Options to Improve the Efficacy of Preferential Duty Programs

The next Administration could pursue several reforms at both the administrative and legislative levels to maximize the efficacy of the preferential duty programs in promoting worker rights abroad.

1. Information Gathering and Resource Development

The U.S. government needs to increase its ability to monitor the observance of internationally recognized worker rights abroad. Currently, the Trade Policy Staff Committee must rely almost exclusively on labor attachés in U.S. embassies to provide the information on which review determinations under the GSP and initial designation decisions under the CBI must be made.[95] The ability of these attachés to obtain reliable information is constrained in many cases by limited resources and restrictions imposed by the governments under review. While additional resource allocations would surely assist the State Department in collecting the information necessary to make a fair determination in each case, these resources alone would not lead to more effective information gathering in situations where governments refuse to cooperate in the inquiries or even to grant the labor attachés access to industrial centers within the beneficiary countries. This problem could be addressed by a statutory or administrative requirement that all beneficiary countries provide the labor attachés with reasonable access to industrial facilities and, where warranted, detention facilities,[96] as a condition of participation in the GSP program.

---

95. Moreover, in many of the smaller beneficiary countries, the U.S. embassy is not even staffed with a labor attaché. In such cases the embassy must rely on labor reporting officers or, if none is assigned to the Embassy, to general foreign service officers.

96. One violation frequently cited by worker rights petitioners is the unjust imprisonment of labor organizers or union members.

The next Administration should also consider organizing a formal advisory committee within its official system for receiving advice from private sector representatives. Short of that, it could better utilize the independent network of labor and human rights organizations to assist the Trade Policy Staff Committee in collecting information regarding worker rights abroad and in lending technical assistance to countries that wish to improve their worker rights performance. By drawing upon the resources and expertise of such organizations as the International Labor Organization, Amnesty International, the International Confederation of Free Trade Unions, the Lawyers Committee for Human Rights and so forth, the U.S. government could supplement its current knowledge of worker rights practices at little extra expense.

2. Procedural Reforms Concerning the GSP Annual Review Process

a. Clarify the GSP Regulations

The next Administration should promulgate a more comprehensive regulation concerning the administration of worker rights petitions during the GSP Annual Review process. The regulation should clarify the standards the Trade Policy Staff Committee will apply in each phase of the review process and should specify the party or parties that must bear the burden of persuasion. This clarification would be particularly beneficial with regard to Phase One determinations. As noted earlier,[97] the present regulation would appear to compel the President's acceptance of all petitions that are facially complete and that present information concerning a beneficiary country not subjected to a previous review concerning worker rights practices or that present substantially new information concerning a country that has been previously reviewed. The Reagan Administration however, has rejected a number of petitions in Phase One for unexplained reasons or for reasons not grounded in the GSP statute or regulation. While there may be a well-founded concern of the Committee that the Annual Review process not be allowed to lapse into a disruptive country-bashing affair for private parties to publicly air their

---

97. *See supra* text accompanying notes 51-54.

grievances unrelated to worker rights, the next Administration could develop more precise methods of screening out frivolous and bad-faith petitions that are not grounded in genuine worker rights violations than the current practice of summarily rejecting undesirable petitions without a public explanation for the agency's decision.

b. Formalize the Procedures by Which the USTR Publicizes the Determinations of the President Following Worker Rights Review Proceedings

Currently, the Trade Policy Staff Committee (via the USTR) issues only terse and conclusory press releases concerning the results of its General and Annual Reviews of worker rights. The agency rarely explains in a conspicuous manner the President's Phase One determinations concerning the acceptance of worker rights petitions. Often the USTR's press release will fail to address many of the petitioner's central allegations concerning worker rights violations. In addition to denying a fair adjudication of the petitioner's claims, this administrative practice fails to offer clear guidance to potential petitioners and respondent beneficiary countries alike as to what factors the agency considers relevant in making worker rights determinations. Further, the practice fails to provide Congress with an adequate basis to oversee the administration of the worker rights provision.

In light of these concerns, the next Administration should amend the GSP regulation to compel the USTR to explain fully the legal and factual bases of the President's decisions at both stages of the worker rights review and to publish these opinions in the *Federal Register*.

c. Provide for Increased Public Participation in the Review Process

To the extent possible, the next Administration should attempt to open the review process to public participation and review. At present, the public is allowed only to petition the Trade Policy Staff Committee for review and to attend scheduled review hearings conducted in the fall. Most of the agency's documentation of worker rights practices in beneficiary countries and virtually all of its deliberations that lead to final recommendations are never made available for public inspection. To be sure, there is a legitimate need to maintain some degree of confidentiality in these reviews to preserve the integrity of the United States' diplomatic relationships and to protect the safety of those individuals living within the countries under review who cooperate with the Committee's investigation. The rather strict degree of secrecy encompassing the current review proceedings, however, tends to minimize the potentially beneficial impact these reviews can have upon international worker rights practices, particularly in countries that are concerned about maintaining a favorable international reputation concerning worker rights and human rights practices. By opening up the review proceedings to allow for increased public participation and review, the next Administration could maximize the benefits of public exposure upon the practice of foreign governments. Perhaps the first step the next Administration could take in this regard would be to require the Committee to maintain a non-confidential record of each investigation that would be available for public inspection and distribution.

d. Relocate the Decisionmaking Authority

As an even broader reform measure, the next Administration should consider removing the authority for making actual worker rights determinations from the Trade Policy Staff Committee to the Departments of State and/or Labor which historically have shown a greater sensitivity and expertise in areas relating to human rights and worker rights. Under one such scheme, the Committee would be compelled to remove a country from the program where the State Department had found that the country's government was not taking sufficient steps to accord its workers the enumerated worker rights.

3. Substantive Reforms Concerning the Administration of the GSP Program

a. Review the Worker Rights Practices of All Beneficiary Developing Countries

At present, the Trade Policy Staff Committee reviews only the worker rights practices of countries against which petitions have been filed. The President could instead require the Committee to review the worker rights status of *all* beneficiary countries during the GSP's Annual Review process, even in the absence of worker rights petitions filed by interested parties. The President could also require the Committee to shift the burden of proof with respect to the central issue of the provision of worker rights to the governments of the beneficiary countries themselves which are in a better strategic and financial position than human rights organizations to supply the Committee with pertinent information concerning the provision of worker rights within the country.

b. Broaden the Scope of Violations That Could Result in Termination from the GSP Program

In light of the Trade Policy Staff Committee's difficult experience in differentiating between "worker rights" and "human rights," the next Administration should consider recommending to the Congress that the GSP statute be amended to include the denial of *human rights*[98] as a basis for termination from the GSP program. This reform would give the Administration a legal basis to deny preferential trade benefits to those governments that commit egregious violations of human rights but whose victims cannot be tied directly to labor activities. There is no longer any rational policy basis for making distinctions between violations of narrowly defined worker rights and more fundamental human rights violations such as abduction, torture and murder. Foreign governments that commit or encourage such activities are not entitled to preferential duty treatment.

c. Reconsider the Reagan Administration's Determinations in Certain Previous Reviews

The next Administration should reconsider the determinations made by President Reagan in a number of worker rights petitions filed by human rights organizations in the 1985-1986 General Review and the 1987 Annual Review.

---

98. As defined in Section 116(a) of the Foreign Assistance Act of 1961, as amended, 22 U.S.C.A. § 2151n(a). *See* note 63 *supra*.

Such reconsideration could take place by petition during the 1989 Annual Review or by the Trade Policy Staff Committee at its own discretion. It is likely that several of the governments named by those petitions (*e.g.*, Haiti, El Salvador) would merit removal from the program under an objective standard that is consistent with the GSP statute.

4. Review of CBI Beneficiaries

The next Administration and Congress should also consider revising the CBI program to include periodic reviews of worker rights practices and the possibility of premature termination of CBI benefits to beneficiary countries due to worker rights violations. Such a revision would be necessary to close an unintended loophole in the worker rights provision of the GSP program. The benefits accorded by the GSP and CBI programs now operate independently of one another. Many articles from countries with poor worker rights records (such as El Salvador and Haiti) are presently designated to receive duty-free entry under both the GSP and the CBI. Even if Haiti, for example, were to be terminated from the GSP program due to worker rights violations, this action would not affect its status as a CBI beneficiary. Under current administrative practice, many of the Haitian articles previously eligible for duty-free entry under the GSP would remain eligible for the same preferential treatment under the CBI. The independent administration of the CBI without periodic eligibility review potentially neutralizes the effect of a revocation of GSP benefits due to worker rights violations.

5. A Refined Approach to Preferential Duty Programs and Worker Rights

The advantages of conditioning preferential duty treatment on respect for fundamental worker rights are twofold. First, these provisions allow the United States to take a moral stand against the world's worst violators of worker rights and human rights by simply denying them any access to preferential trade benefits. This is perhaps the appropriate approach with respect to those few regimes whose violations are so egregious and systemic that no amount of trade benefits will induce any measurable respect on their part for the rights of human beings.[99]

Second, and perhaps more importantly, these provisions create opportunities for the United States government to develop and use its leverage on several levels to promote improved respect for worker rights by the majority of the governments of beneficiary countries that are interested in securing favorable trade and diplomatic relationships with the United States. By developing and supporting both governmental and non-governmental organizations to monitor worker rights practices and to assist interested countries in improving labor standards, the U.S. government can supplement its diplomatic efforts to encourage democratic reforms in the foreign workplace.

In addition to enlisting the support of the international worker rights and human rights communities, the next Administration could seek the assistance of progressive elements of the United States business community, particularly those involved in retail trade, in forming a new national policy concerning the procurement of goods from abroad. The Administration should encourage the business community to enter into voluntary covenants to insist on minimum respect for worker rights by foreign governments whose countries supply their products.[100] Such agreements could help reduce the current pressure on governments of beneficiary countries to suppress worker rights in order to attract foreign investment.

Finally, the United States must take the lead in proving to the beneficiary countries that worker rights and economic development are not inversely related to one another, but rather that the provision of worker rights is essential toward developing strong internal markets to reduce the dependence on

---

99. In saying this, we applaud and endorse the Reagan Administration's decision to remove beneficiary countries such as Chile, Paraguay and Romania from the GSP program.

100. The European Economic Community currently incorporates minimum labor standards into several of its commodity agreements.

export income and toward creating the highly-skilled workforces necessary to lead the economies of beneficiary countries beyond the initial stages of economic development.

To be sure, the next Administration will encounter considerable resistance from many beneficiary countries that feel that they have not yet reached a sufficient level of economic development to be able to afford providing worker rights to their workers and in all events resent the efforts of the United States to determine the appropriate level of labor standards to be provided in their countries. In instances where such a country is particularly resistant to negotiated reforms, the President should again consider the denial of GSP benefits as a last resort. The GSP statute provides, however, a *variety* of options to an Administration that is concerned about worker rights violations in a particular country but which does not wish to terminate completely the country's participation in a program that encourages economic growth and development and that ultimately seeks to improve the welfare of its workers. In such instances the President could instruct the USTR to impose less restrictive penalties against the country such as (1) the removal of specifically designated articles produced by industries or companies where the most egregious worker rights violations were found to occur, or (2) the reduction of the competitive need limits on certain articles imported from the country. These options will provide the next Administration with the flexibility necessary to advance worker rights while taking into account political and diplomatic considerations that militate against the imposition of broad trade sanctions in particular cases.

A further option available to the President is a complete waiver of GSP sanctions in cases where he determines that this is in the national economic interest of the United States.[101] In these instances, we recommend that the Trade Policy Staff Committee be allowed to complete the worker rights review process and make a public determination that the country at issue is not affording its workers internationally recognized worker rights before the President exercises his waiver authority. In such instances, it may be important to preserve the benefits arising from public awareness of and participation

---

101. 19 U.S.C.A. § 2464(c)(3)(A).

in the worker rights review despite the eventual waiver of sanctions.

III. SECTION 301 OF THE TRADE ACT OF 1974

Section 301 of the Trade Act of 1974[102] is the least definitive and one of the most internationally sensitive of the United States' import trade relief statutes. Section 301 authorizes the President, through the USTR,[103] to enter into negotiations with foreign governments to seek the elimination of trade barriers and other "unfair trade practices." When negotiations and international mediation fail to bring the foreign government's objectionable trade practice or practices to an end, Section 301 grants the President broad discretionary authority to impose retaliatory trade sanctions that restrict U.S. market access to that country's products and services.

Section 301 was initially enacted to assist the President in removing foreign trade barriers that denied or impaired the United States' rights under GATT[104] and other trade agreements. More recently, this provision has been used by the Executive to respond to foreign trade practices that, while not expressly prohibited by GATT, nonetheless harm U.S. interests. For example, the Reagan Administration repeatedly initiated proceedings under Section 301 in response to perceived inadequate protection for U.S. intellectual property rights in many developing countries.

Under the Omnibus Trade and Competitiveness Act of 1988,[105] however, Congress has extended the President's

---

102. Pub. L. No. 93-618, 88 Stat. 2066 (1975) codified at 19 U.S.C.A. § 2411 *et seq.* (1980 and West Supp. 1988). "Section 301" refers collectively to sections 301 through 309 (comprising chapter 1 of title III) of the Trade Act of 1974, as amended.

103. In discussing Section 301 herein, "USTR" is often used in place of "the President" since its provisions are directed at the USTR. In practice, the USTR's determinations are arrived at through interagency consultations. The ultimate authority for these determinations, moreover, lies with the President.

104. *See* note 18 *supra.*

105. Pub. L. No. 100-418, 102 Stat. 1107 (1988) [hereinafter Omnibus Trade Act].

discretionary authority under Section 301 to impose trade sanctions against foreign governments found to violate fundamental worker rights. The amendments to Section 301 concerning the provision of worker rights abroad reflect the same concerns as those which led to the incorporation of worker rights in the United States' preferential duty programs[106] and in the Overseas Private Investment Corporation Amendment Act of 1985.[107] In addition to the United States' concern for the legitimate rights of foreign workers, it is also widely viewed in this country that the denial of fundamental rights to workers abroad creates an unfair cost advantage in favor of the foreign goods that are produced under repressive conditions and that these practices threaten the economic well-being of workers and responsible employers in the United States.[108] Thus, the U.S. legislation concerning the provision of worker rights abroad seeks primarily to assist foreign workers in achieving better wages and working conditions and in doing so, to reduce the adverse impact on U.S. firms arising from the denial of worker rights by foreign competitors.

Unlike the rather limited preferential duty programs discussed earlier in this memorandum, Section 301 involves a broad grant of discretionary authority to the President to negotiate worker rights agreements with foreign countries and to impose virtually unlimited trade sanctions against *any* foreign country found to deny or impair worker rights. As such, Section 301 creates considerable economic leverage for the U.S. government to apply in promoting respect for worker rights abroad. Further, the legislation allows the United States to take a strong moral stand against the most egregious violators of worker rights by imposing draconian restrictions on the access of those countries' products and services to the U.S. market. Finally, the legislation allows the President to specifically offset

---

106. *See supra* discussion in Part II of the Generalized System of Preferences and the Caribbean Basin Initiative.

107. Pub. L. No. 99-204, 99 Stat. 1670 (1985), codified at 22 U.S.C.A. § 2191 *et seq.* (West Supp. 1988). *See also supra* text accompanying notes 12-16.

108. *Senate Workers' Rights Hearing, supra* note 1, at 38 (statement of Rep. Donald J. Pease).

the unfair trade advantage obtained by producers in foreign countries whose governments deny or restrict fundamental worker rights. The President would have to use this authority judiciously, however, since any sanctions imposed against foreign governments under these laws would raise serious issues concerning the consistency of such action with the United States' obligations under the major multilateral agreement governing world trade.

A. The President's Authority under Section 301

Section 301, as amended, defines two categories of unfair trade practices: those requiring mandatory retaliation and those against which the President may retaliate at his discretion.

1. Mandatory Action

Under the amended Section 301(a), the President must retaliate against a foreign country if the USTR determines that:

(A) the rights of the United States under any trade agreement are being denied; or

(B) an act, policy, or practice of a foreign country--

(i) violates, or is inconsistent with, the provisions of, or otherwise denies benefits to the United States under, any trade agreement, or

(ii) is unjustifiable and burdens or restricts United States commerce.[109]

---

109. Trade Act of 1974, § 301(a), *amended by* the Omnibus Trade Act, *supra* note 105, at § 1301 (to be codified at 19 U.S.C. § 2411[a]). Under the revised Section 301, an act, policy or practice is "unjustifiable" if it violates, or is inconsistent with, the international legal rights of the United States. Acts, policies and practices that are unjustifiable include, but are not limited to, those which deny national or most-favored-nation treatment or the right of establishment or protection of intellectual (continued...)

The USTR is not required to retaliate in these instances, however, if a dispute resolution panel of GATT determines that the rights of the United States under the Agreement are not being denied[110] or if the USTR determines that:

> (A) the foreign country is taking satisfactory measures to grant the rights of the United States under a trade agreement,
>
> (B) the foreign country has-
>
> (i) agreed to eliminate or phase out the act, policy, or practice, or
>
> (ii) agreed to an imminent solution to the burden or restriction on United States commerce that is satisfactory to the [USTR],
>
> (C) it is impossible for the foreign country to achieve the results described in clause (A) or (B), as appropriate, but the foreign country agrees to provide to the United States compensatory trade benefits that are satisfactory to the [USTR],
>
> (D) in extraordinary cases, where the taking of action under this subsection would have an adverse impact on the United States economy substantially out of proportion to the benefits of such action, taking into account the impact of not taking such action on the credibility of the provisions of this chapter, or

---

109. (...continued)
property rights. Trade Act of 1974, § 301(d)(4), *as amended by* the Omnibus Trade Act, *supra* note 105, at § 1301 (to be codified at 19 U.S.C. § 2411[d][4]).

110. Trade Act of 1974, § 301(a)(2)(A), *amended by* the Omnibus Trade Act, *supra* note 105, at § 1301 (to be codified at 19 U.S.C. § 2411[a][2][A]).

(E) the taking of action under this subsection would cause serious harm to the national security of the United States.[111]

Section 301(a)(3), as amended, also mandates that any retaliatory action taken by the USTR under this section to eliminate the unfair foreign trade act be "devised so as to affect goods or services of the foreign country in an amount that is equivalent in value to the burden or restriction being imposed by that country on United States commerce."[112]

2. Discretionary Authority to Respond to the Denial of Internationally Recognized Worker Rights and Other Unfair Trade Practices

Under Section 301(b), the President has discretionary authority to negotiate with and, if necessary, to retaliate against, a foreign government whose act, policy, or practice is "unreasonable or discriminatory[[113]] and burdens or restricts United States commerce" in order to obtain the elimination of that act, policy, or practice.[114] The Omnibus Trade Act incorporates the denial of internationally recognized worker rights into the definition of "unreasonable" acts, policies, or practices that the President may respond to under Section 301.

---

111. Trade Act of 1974, § 301(a)(2)(B), *amended by* the Omnibus Trade Act, *supra* note 105, at § 1301 (to be codified at 19 U.S.C. § 2411[a][2][B]).

112. Trade Act of 1974, § 301(a)(3), *amended by* the Omnibus Trade Act, *supra* note 105, at § 1301 (to be codified at 19 U.S.C. § 2411[a][3]).

113. Acts, policies and practices that are *discriminatory* include, when appropriate, any act, policy and practice which denies national or most-favored-nation treatment to United States goods, services or investment. Trade Act of 1974, § 301(d)(5), *amended by* the Omnibus Trade Act, *supra* note 105, at § 1301 (to be codified at 19 U.S.C. § 2411[d][5]).

114. Trade Act of 1974, § 301(b), *amended by* the Omnibus Trade Act, *supra* note 105, § 1301 (to be codified at 19 U.S.C. § 2411[b]).

Under Section 301(d)(3), as amended:

(A) An act, policy, or practice is unreasonable if the act, policy, or practice, while not necessarily in violation of, or inconsistent with, the international legal rights of the United States, is otherwise unfair and inequitable.

(B) Acts, policies, and practices that are unreasonable include, but are not limited to, any act, policy, or practice, or any combination of any acts, policies, or practices, which . . .

(iii) constitutes a persistent pattern of conduct that-

(I) denies workers the right of association,

(II) denies workers the right to organize and bargain collectively,

(III) permits any form of forced or compulsory labor,

(IV) fails to provide a minimum age for the employment of children, or

(V) fails to provide standards for minimum wages, hours of work, and occupational safety and health of workers.[115]

---

115. Trade Act of 1974 § 301(d)(3), *amended by* the Omnibus Trade Act, *supra* note 105, at § 1301 (to be codified at 19 U.S.C. § 2411[d][3]). The definition of worker rights in Section 301 parallels the definition contained in the GSP program, discussed *supra.* Other trade practices considered *unreasonable* within the meaning of Section 301 include export targeting and the denial of intellectual property rights. Trade Act of 1974, §301(d)(3)(B)(i), (ii), *amended by* the Omnibus Trade Act, *supra* note 105, at § 1301 (to be codified at 19 U.S.C. § 2411[d][3][B][i], [ii]).

Under Section 301(d)(3)(C)(i), however, the President may not retaliate against the foreign country if the USTR determines that-

> (I) the foreign country has taken, or is taking, actions that demonstrate a significant and tangible overall advancement in providing throughout the foreign country (including any designated zone within the foreign country) the rights and other standards described in the subclauses of subparagraph (B)(iii), or
>
> (II) such acts, policies, and practices are not inconsistent with the level of economic development of the foreign country.

B. Procedures for Review of Unfair Trade Practices (Including the Denial of Internationally Recognized Worker Rights) under Section 301

The application of Section 301 to the unfair trade practices of a foreign government normally entails a lengthy administrative process conducted by the USTR. A Section 301 proceeding involves investigation, consultation, negotiation with the foreign government involved, referral to the GATT dispute resolution process[116] and, if such efforts fail, a recommendation to the President from the USTR concerning what trade sanctions, if any, should be imposed against the foreign government. Most disputes involving Section 301 are resolved through negotiations and the actual imposition of trade sanctions under this law is uncommon.[117] Under the Omnibus Trade Act,

---

116. A dispute that is the subject of a petition under Section 301 would normally be referred to GATT when the respondent country is also a GATT signatory.

117. *See, e.g.*, Canada Border Broadcasting, Office of the USTR Docket No. 301-15, 45 Fed. Reg. 51,173 (1980) (Reagan Administration proposed mirror legislation concerning broadcasting restriction rather than trade sanctions under Section (continued...)

worker rights reviews would be conducted by the USTR under the same procedures as those involving reviews of other unfair trade practices.

1. Initiation of Investigations

The USTR has authority under Section 302(b) to initiate investigations concerning unfair trade practices on its own motion.[118] Further, Section 302(a)(1), as amended, allows "[a]ny interested person"[119] to file a petition with the USTR requesting

---

117. (...continued)
301); EC Pasta Export Subsidies, Office of the USTR Docket No. 301-25, 50 Fed. Reg. 26,143, 33,711 (1985); Japan Semiconductors, Office of the USTR Docket No. 301-48, 52 Fed. Reg. 13,412 (1987). *See also* Unfair Trade Practices: Brazil's Lack of Adequate Intellectual Property Protection for Pharmaceuticals and Fine Chemicals (Investigation under Section 301 of the Trade Act of 1974, Notice of Public Hearings and Request for Public Comments), 53 Fed. Reg. 28,100 (1988).

118. Trade Act of 1974, § 302(b), *amended by* the Omnibus Trade Act, *supra* note 105, at § 1301 (to be codified at 19 U.S.C. § 2412[b]).

119. Trade Act of 1974, § 302(a)(1), *amended by* the Omnibus Trade Act, *supra* note 105, at § 1301 (to be codified at 19 U.S.C. § 2412[a][1]). The Omnibus Trade Act does not appear to impose any requirement of standing to file a petition under Section 301 regarding unfair trade practices such as the denial of worker rights. The Act does contain a somewhat restrictive definition of "interested persons" for purposes of requesting a public hearing following the initiation of a Section 301 investigation by the USTR. For purposes of requesting a public hearing or an alternative "opportunity for the presentation of views" under Sections 302(a)(4)(B), 304(b)(1)(A), 306(c)(2) or 307(a)(2) only, Section 301(d)(9) defines the term "interested persons" as including, but not limited to, "domestic firms and workers, representatives of consumer interests, United States product exporters, and any industrial user of any goods or services that may be affected by actions taken under [Section 301]." Trade Act of 1974, § 301(d)(9), *amended by* the Omnibus
(continued...)

that action be taken under Section 301. Upon the filing of a petition by an interested party, the USTR reviews the petitioner's allegations and, not later than 45 days after the date on which the USTR has received the petition, determines whether to initiate an investigation.

If the USTR determines to initiate an investigation regarding the issues raised in the petition, the agency must publish a summary of the petition in the *Federal Register* and must thereafter provide for the presentation of views concerning the issues raised in the petition, including a public hearing, if requested by an interested party.[120] If the USTR determines not to initiate an investigation, the USTR must inform the petitioner of the reasons therefor and must publish a notice of the determination, together with a summary of the reasons therefor, in the *Federal Register*.

2. Consultation and Referral Upon Initiation of Investigation

Once the USTR determines to initiate an investigation, the agency must request consultations with the foreign country concerned regarding the issues involved in the investigation.[121] If the USTR and the foreign government are able to reach an agreement concerning improved worker rights practices in that country, Section 301 authorizes the USTR to enter into binding agreements with the foreign country that commit the country to eliminate or phase out the objectionable labor policies or practices, to eliminate any burden or restriction on U.S. commerce resulting from worker rights violations, or to provide

---

119. (...continued)
Trade Act, *supra* note 105, at § 1301 (to be codified at 19 U.S.C. § 2411[d][9]).

120. Trade Act of 1974, § 302(a)(4), *amended by* the Omnibus Trade Act, *supra* note 105, at § 1301 (to be codified at 19 U.S.C. § 2412[a][4]).

121. Trade Act of 1974, § 303(a)(1), *amended by* the Omnibus Trade Act, *supra* note 105, at § 1301 (to be codified at 19 U.S.C. § 2413[a][1]).

the United States with compensatory trade benefits in lieu of improved worker rights practices.[122]

Normally, if a Section 301 investigation involves a trade agreement (such as GATT) and a mutually acceptable resolution is not reached through bilateral negotiations within 150 days following the commencement of consultation or the close of the consultation period, if any, as specified in the trade agreement, the USTR must request proceedings on the matter under GATT's formal dispute settlement procedures.[123] A worker rights investigation under Section 301, however, would not be subject to referral to GATT since the Agreement does not impose worker rights obligations upon its signatories.[124] As a result, any negotiations or consultations undertaken between the United States and the country under review would have to be conducted on a strictly bilateral basis.[125]

---

122. Trade Act of 1974, § 301(c)(1)(C), *amended by* the Omnibus Trade Act, *supra* note 105, at § 1301 (to be codified at 19 U.S.C. § 2411[c][1][C]). While Section 301 is structured so as to allow foreign governments to maintain their unfair trade practices by granting compensatory trade benefits to U.S. exporters, it is doubtful that such a resolution would be appropriate in a dispute involving worker rights since the compensatory trade benefits would do nothing to improve the position of workers in the exporting country nor would such benefits operate to mitigate the unfair trade advantage obtained by the foreign producers that deny worker rights.

123. Trade Act of 1974, § 303(a)(2), *amended by* the Omnibus Trade Act, *supra* note 105, at § 1301 (to be codified at 19 U.S.C. § 2413[a][2]).

124. *See infra* text accompanying notes 143-146.

125. As discussed *infra*, however, the United States' actual imposition of trade sanctions under Section 301 against a fellow GATT signatory due to worker rights practices would likely be referred to GATT since the U.S. action would certainly impair the other signatory's right to most-favored-nation treatment under Article 1 of GATT.

3. Final Determinations by the USTR

If the consultations and proceedings held under Section 303 do not lead to a resolution of the dispute, the USTR must make a final determination whether (1) the rights of the United States under any trade agreement are being denied, or (2) any unreasonable, unjustifiable or discriminatory act, policy or practice (including the denial of worker rights) exists.[126] An affirmative final determination that a foreign government is committing an unfair trade practice that burdens U.S. commerce is the legal prerequisite for the imposition of retaliatory trade sanctions under Section 301, discussed below.

Section 304(a)(2) sets time limits for the USTR's final determinations concerning unfair trade practices under Section 304(a)(1). In worker rights proceedings, as in most other investigations, the USTR must make a final determination within twelve months following the initiation of the investigation.[127] With respect to worker rights, if the USTR determines under Section 301(d)(3)(C)(i)[128] that the foreign government under review is making significant advancements in providing worker rights and is therefore not committing an unfair trade practice, the USTR is required to publish this determination in the *Federal Register* together with a

---

126. Trade Act of 1974, § 304(a)(1), *amended by* the Omnibus Trade Act, *supra* note 105, at § 1301 (to be codified at 19 U.S.C. § 2414[a][1]).

127. The statute sets alternative time limits for USTR determinations in investigations involving trade agreements [Section 304(a)(2)(A)], investigations involving "complex or complicated issues . . . that require additional time" [Section 304(a)(3)(B)(i)], and investigations concerning the provision of intellectual property rights by foreign governments [Sections 304(a)(3)(B)(ii) and (iii)].

128. Trade Act of 1974, § 301(d)(3)(C)(i), *amended by* the Omnibus Trade Act, *supra* note 105, at § 1301 (to be codified at 19 U.S.C. § 2411[d][3][C][i]).

description of the underlying facts.[129] If the determination is affirmative, *i.e.*, if the USTR determines the foreign government under review is denying internationally recognized worker rights to its workers, the USTR must also determine what trade sanctions, if any, to impose against the offending country.[130]

Before making its final determination and recommendations, however, the USTR, unless expeditious action is required, must provide an opportunity for the presentation of views by interested persons, including a public hearing if requested by any interested person.[131] The agency may also request the views of the United States International Trade Commission regarding the probable impact on the U.S. economy if action is taken with respect to any goods or services.[132]

C. Retaliatory Trade Measures Authorized by Section 301

If the USTR determines that a foreign government is violating worker rights and negotiations with the government of that country fail to produce any commitment concerning increased respect for such rights, the amended Section 301 provides a wide variety of trade sanctions that the President may impose alternatively or in combination against the offending country. Specifically, the President may:

---

129. Trade Act of 1974, § 301(d)(3)(C)(ii), *amended by* the Omnibus Trade Act, *supra* note 105, at § 1301 (to be codified at 19 U.S.C. § 2411[d][3][C][ii]).

130. Trade Act of 1974, § 301(a)(1)(B), *amended by* the Omnibus Trade Act, *supra* note 105, at § 1301 (to be codified at 19 U.S.C. § 2414[a][1][B]).

131. Trade Act of 1974, § 304(b)(1)(A), *amended by* the Omnibus Trade Act, *supra* note 105, at § 1301 (to be codified at 19 U.S.C. § 2414[b][1][A]).

132. Trade Act of 1974, § 304(b)(1)(C), *amended by* the Omnibus Trade Act, *supra* note 105, at § 1301 (to be codified at 19 U.S.C. § 2414[b][1][C]).

> A. suspend, withdraw, or prevent the application of, benefits of trade agreement concessions to carry out a trade agreement with the foreign country . . . .;
>
> B. impose duties or other import restrictions on the goods of, and, notwithstanding any other provision of law, fees or restrictions on the services of, such foreign country for such time as [the President] determines appropriate.[133]

The President is also authorized to impose restrictions on the provision of services in the United States by firms based in the offending country.[134] Further, Section 301 allows the President to impose sanctions against specific goods or services originating in the offending country "without regard to whether or not such goods or services were involved in the act, policy, or practice that is the subject of such action."[135]

D. Potential Problems with the Enforcement of the Worker Rights Provisions of Section 301

The Reagan Administration made it clear to Congress in 1987 that it opposed the amendment of Section 301 to incorporate the denial of internationally recognized worker rights as an unfair trade practice.[136] While much of the Administration's criticism stemmed from its general disfavor of the incorporation of worker rights into U.S. trade law or policy, many of the specific arguments put forth by the Administration in opposition to the Section 301 amendments nonetheless deserve

---

133. Trade Act of 1974, § 301(c)(1)(A) and (B), *amended by* the Omnibus Trade Act, *supra* note 105, at § 1301 (to be codified at 19 U.S.C. § 2411[c][1][A] and [B]).

134. Trade Act of 1974, § 301(c)(2), *amended by* the Omnibus Trade Act, *supra* note 105, at § 1301 (to be codified at 19 U.S.C. § 2411[c][2]).

135. Trade Act of 1974, § 301(c)(3)(B), *amended by* the Omnibus Trade Act, *supra* note 105, at § 1301 (to be codified at 19 U.S.C. § 2414[c][3][B]).

136. *See* Smith Statement, *supra* note 19, at 51.

serious consideration by policymakers interested in promoting worker rights through trade legislation.

1. Inconsistency with United States' Obligations under the General Agreement on Tariffs and Trade

The inclusion of a foreign country's denial of internationally recognized worker rights as an unfair trade practice under Section 301 raises serious issues concerning the United States' international obligations under multilateral trade agreements, particularly GATT. GATT is subscribed to by over eighty-five governments which together account for more than four-fifths of the world's trade[137] and is the only multilateral agreement that defines generally accepted rules for international trade.[138] GATT also functions as the principal multilateral forum for negotiating the reduction of trade barriers and the liberalization of trade worldwide.

The paramount principle of GATT to which all signatories must adhere is embodied in the most-favored-nation (MFN) clause[139] which prohibits discriminatory trade and tariff practices. Under GATT, all contracting parties are bound to grant each other treatment as favorable as they give to any other country with regard to import and export duties. No signatory may give special trading advantages to another and all

---

137. U.S. TRADE REPRESENTATIVE, A PREFACE TO TRADE (1982) (available from the Office of the U.S. Trade Representative) [hereinafter PREFACE TO TRADE].

138. Alleged violations of GATT rules may be resolved through a formal dispute resolution process which is quite lengthy. *See* GATT, *supra* note 18, Art. 22. If upon review, a GATT panel determines that a signatory has breached its obligations under GATT, the signatory may ultimately forfeit its rights under the Agreement. Many signatories, however, maintain legal mechanisms to enforce their rights under GATT through unilateral retaliation against any signatory they believe has breached its obligations under the Agreement. The United States' mechanism for such unilateral retaliation is Section 301.

139. GATT, *supra* note 18, Art. 1.

contracting parties must share equally in the reduction of trade barriers.[140]

GATT creates exceptions to the MFN rule only in limited circumstances. For example, a signatory may impose additional duties on imports from another signatory if the government of the importing country determines that the government of the exporting country is providing subsidies[141] to its exporters, or that the producer(s) in the exporting country are "dumping"[142] their products abroad. GATT also allows each signatory to take "any action which it considers necessary for the protection of its essential security interests . . . taken in time of war or other emergency in international relations."[143] With the possible exception of a waiver of the MFN clause concerning the importation of articles produced by prison labor,[144] GATT does not recognize the denial of internationally recognized worker rights by one signatory as an unlawful trade practice.

The legal difficulty with the enforcement of the new worker rights provision of Section 301 is that the United States would have no substantive basis under GATT to take retaliatory trade action against another GATT signatory because of that country's labor practices. It would likely be disingenuous for the United States to construe GATT's silence on worker rights as an indication that the original signatories intended to suspend MFN treatment on the basis of worker rights since the United States itself unsuccessfully attempted to raise the issue of worker

---

140. PREFACE TO TRADE, *supra* note 137, at 5.

141. GATT, *supra* note 18, Arts. 6 and 16. The United States countervailing duty law that applies to GATT signatories is codified at 19 U.S.C.A. § 1671 *et seq.* (1980 and West Supp. 1988).

142. GATT, *supra* note 18, Art. 6. Dumping is the sale of an article by an exporting producer at less than that product's "fair market value." *See* 19 U.S.C.A. § 1673 *et seq.* (1980 and West Supp. 1988).

143. GATT, *supra* note 18, Art. 21.

144. *See* GATT, *supra* note 18, Art. 20(e).

rights with its trading partners at the GATT in 1986. The U.S. delegation sought to include a discussion of worker rights in the pending round of multilateral trade negotiations which began at Punta del Este, Uruguay in 1986. At the ministerial conference held in September of that year, the U.S. delegation attempted to form a working group to discuss worker rights during the Uruguay Round. The U.S. efforts to secure the necessary consensus for the working group were unsuccessful, however, primarily because the majority of developing countries currently view the efforts of the United States and other developed countries to infuse international labor standards into GATT as a "Trojan horse for protectionism."[145]

Without an internationally recognized basis on which to impose trade sanctions, any United States action under Section 301 to address the denial of worker rights by a fellow signatory would appear to constitute a substantive violation of GATT's MFN clause, or at least a procedural evasion of GATT's dispute resolution mechanism. Such an action by the United States could invite retaliatory trade action by the other signatory and its allies.[146]

Notwithstanding these concerns, however, the United States' imposition of trade sanctions against GATT signatories without explicit authority under GATT is not without precedent. For instance, the USTR's investigations against certain developing countries under Section 301 concerning inadequate protection of intellectual property rights has no basis in GATT and any sanction imposed against such countries would appear to violate the MFN provision of Article 1 of GATT. The U.S. government's proffered rationale behind these proceedings is that since the inadequate protection of intellectual property rights does not come within the purview of GATT (*i.e.*, trade in goods), GATT does not apply to such proceedings. A similar rationale is applied to cases where the United States has considered restricting the importation of goods from countries whose governments refuse to permit U.S. firms to compete in their domestic service markets.

---

145. *See* Smith Statement, *supra* note 19, at 57.

146. *Id.*

2. Difficulties in Quantifying the Burden on U.S. Commerce

Another enforcement challenge confronting the USTR would be a determination as to the "burden or restriction on U.S. commerce" created by the denial of worker rights abroad. The "burden" to U.S. commerce in the case of worker rights practices is the unfair competitive advantage obtained by foreign producers over U.S. producers of competing merchandise. By denying worker rights, certain foreign producers are able to reduce their labor costs and sell their goods in foreign markets, such as the United States, at prices considerably below the "fair market value" that U.S. and other producers that respect worker rights must charge in order to remain profitable. The result, of course, is a loss of sales and jobs to the United States industries producing goods similar to those produced under repressive labor conditions abroad.

Although Section 301 does not impose any quantitative obligations[147] on foreign producers, it is generally presumed by supporters of worker rights legislation that the provision of qualitative worker rights, such as freedom of association and the right to organize and bargain collectively, would inevitably result in increased wages and benefits to foreign workers. Foreign producers, faced with increased labor costs, would pass along at least a portion of these costs in the form of higher prices to their importers in the United States. This in turn would raise the wholesale prices of the foreign products to a level approaching that with which U.S. producers could fairly compete.

The challenge facing the USTR in those worker rights proceedings where negotiations between the United States and the foreign government have failed to reach an agreement concerning worker rights will be to *quantify* the extent of the unfair trade advantage in terms of a "social dumping" margin;

---

147. Examples of quantitative obligations include the payment of specific minimum wages, the provision of unemployment or health insurance to employees, and occupational safety and health standards.

i.e., the unfair price advantage (expressed as a percentage of the product's value) obtained by the foreign producers operating in countries that deny worker rights.

While Section 301 currently offers no guidance to the USTR as to how the agency must attempt to quantify the price and cost effects of worker rights violations, the agency could possibly apply a form of "constructed value" analysis, similar to that employed by the Department of Commerce in antidumping proceedings[148] to estimate the likely impact on cost and prices of the foreign goods under review if the government of that country were to afford internationally recognized labor rights to its workers. The USTR could begin its fair value assessment by selecting a surrogate economy comparable in economic development to the country under review, but one in which workers enjoy the internationally recognized labor rights detailed in Section 301. By examining the costs of production or wholesale prices of articles produced in the appropriate surrogate country, the USTR could determine the fair value of similar goods produced in the country under review. The difference between the fair value and the prices charged by producers in the country under review would constitute the margin of "social dumping" and would provide a basis upon which the USTR could assess offsetting duties under Section 301(c)(1)(B). It must be conceded, however, that any

---

148. *See* 19 U.S.C.A. § 1677b(e) (1980 and West Supp. 1988). The USTR could work in conjunction with the Department of Commerce in conducting a constructed value analysis similar to that employed in antidumping proceedings brought against producers in non-market economies. In such antidumping proceedings, the Department of Commerce determines the foreign products' fair market value by examining the cost of production and price data from producers in selected "surrogate" countries which the Department of Commerce considers to be at a comparable level of economic development with the non-market economy under review. *See* 19 U.S.C.A. §1677b(c), 19 C.F.R. § 353.8 (1988).

methodology used by the USTR to arrive at a social dumping margin would necessarily be imprecise.[149]

3. Confrontational Nature of Section 301 Proceedings

Worker rights and human rights issues tend to be highly sensitive politically and diplomatically. Moreover, most foreign governments, particularly those with poor human rights or worker rights records, generally resist any action by the United States that interferes with their "internal affairs." According to Deputy Trade Representative Michael B. Smith, the "[u]se of the very public Section 301 procedure, with its public finding of unfairness, to deal with such complaints would tend to aggravate national sensitivities in such a way as to preclude the sort of evolutionary progress that might be achieved by other, less confrontational means."[150]

E. Conclusion and Recommendations

The revision of Section 301 to incorporate the denial of worker rights as an unfair trade practice provides a potentially potent weapon for the next Administration to apply in advancing worker rights abroad. This authority must be used cautiously, however, so as to avert any undue disruption of the international trade order or potential retaliation by the United States' trading partners. Moreover, it is likely that the actual imposition of trade sanctions under Section 301 against a GATT signatory on the basis of worker rights violations would violate the United States' obligations under GATT. Nevertheless, the amendments to Section 301 create new opportunities for the United States to use its negotiating leverage to reach binding agreements with foreign governments concerning improved

---

149. *See* Smith Statement, *supra* note 19, at 61-62 (discussing the difficulty in quantifying the impact of the denial of worker rights on U.S. commerce).

150. *Id.* at 60 (referring to complaints raised in review proceedings under the GSP concerning violation of worker rights in countries receiving preferential duty treatment under the GSP program).

worker rights practices. Likewise, the United States' legal obligations under GATT do not necessarily preclude the successful initiation of adversarial proceedings under Section 301 to redress worker rights violations abroad, provided the next Administration exercises great care in selecting a target for a worker rights investigation.

1. Enhanced Opportunities for Bilateral Negotiation Efforts

The President has always possessed inherent authority to negotiate treaties and executive agreements with representatives of other nations. The worker rights amendments to Section 301 enhance this authority in two ways. First, the amended Section 301 provides a statutory framework for the negotiations. The foreign government would likely have a substantial incentive to negotiate the improved provision of worker rights in good faith since the U.S. Congress has clearly stated its intent to limit the U.S. market access of producers in countries that deny worker rights. Whether or not these negotiations take place under the auspices of a worker rights proceeding under Section 301, any resulting agreement reached between the United States and one of its trading partners would be enforceable under Sections 301(a) and 301(c)(1)(C).

The United States has undertaken similar negotiating efforts in other areas of trade policy, such as the fields of intellectual property rights, foreign investment restrictions, and U.S. access to foreign services markets. In each case, the United States has sought to negotiate bilateral agreements with those governments whose policies or practices present the greatest burdens upon or obstacles to U.S. commercial activities. In the case of intellectual property for example, the U.S. government has been able to secure a significant number of bilateral agreements with its major Asian trading partners concerning the protection of U.S. patents and copyrights abroad; the United States further hopes that these countries will be co-opted into joining the U.S. efforts in multilateral fora, such as GATT, to create a "level playing field" for all nations with regard to intellectual property protection.

The new Administration could . undertake a similar negotiating effort with regard to creating a level playing field on worker rights. If the U.S. government were able to reach a substantial number of worker rights agreements under the auspices of Section 301, the contracting parties to such agreements would have a strong incentive to support U.S. and other initiatives brought during the course of multilateral trade negotiations. If the United States were to organize a sizable community of nations willing to promote worker rights before the GATT, it is conceivable that such a group would be able to secure a limited waiver of the MFN rule that differentiates GATT signatories on the basis of their adherence to a "worker rights code."[151] While the threat of Section 301 sanctions might underlie the willingness of some of the United States' trading partners to negotiate, none of these negotiating objectives need actually require the imposition of trade sanctions under Section 301 or even the initiation of Section 301 proceedings.

2. Domestic Negotiations and Agreements

While much of the next Administration's efforts in promoting worker rights abroad should be directed at the source of the abuses, some negotiating efforts should be aimed at the domestic retailing community that purchases the goods produced under repressive conditions in foreign countries. The next President should give serious consideration to pursuing an agreement within the U.S. wholesaling and retailing community not to purchase products made in countries that deny worker rights. Such covenants, if properly and effectively monitored by the federal government, would encourage foreign governments to make substantive concessions on labor rights.

---

151. A similar, limited waiver of the MFN rule applies in the case of the GATT Subsidies Code, wherein the products of signatories to the Code are granted an injury test before the government of an importing signatory imposes any countervailing duties. The U.S. countervailing duty law that applies to Subsidies Code signatories is found at 19 U.S.C.A. § 1671 *et seq.* (1980 and West Supp. 1988); the countervailing duty law that applies to non-Subsidies Code signatories is found at 19 U.S.C.A. § 1303 (1980 and West Supp. 1988).

3. Public Relations-Based Incentives to Improve Worker Rights Practices

As detailed earlier in this memorandum,[152] much of the potential benefit arising from a trade-related worker rights proceeding is the public relations impact of such an investigation. Many foreign governments that wish to maintain favorable trade and diplomatic relations with the United States or to avoid being viewed by the international community as human rights violators might respond constructively to a Section 301 investigation in the same way that the governments of Turkey and Thailand responded to the U.S. government's reviews of those countries' worker rights practices under the GSP program. In these cases the United States could use the Section 301 proceeding as an opportunity not merely to use its economic leverage to prod worker rights concessions from recalcitrant trading partners but rather to lend encouragement and technical assistance to governments that seek to improve their worker rights practices.

The incentives to improve worker rights practices arising from the public relations impact of a Section 301 proceeding would likely not apply to many countries that do not maintain close ties to the United States. To the contrary, such countries would likely react in a hostile manner to such an investigation and would label the entire proceeding as a protectionist venture. Further, a Section 301 respondent that was also a GATT signatory would almost surely insist that the United States refer the dispute to the GATT for formal dispute resolution under Article 22. Given the fact that GATT does not expressly mandate respect for worker rights, it is likely that the respondent would prevail against the United States in such a forum. Such a result would clearly detract from the integrity of the Section 301 process and thus underlines the importance of the target-selection process.

4. Making an Example of Egregious Violators

The next Administration could also use Section 301 to make an example of any one of a small number of foreign

---

152. *See supra* text accompanying notes 92-94.

governments whose worker rights and human rights practices are particularly egregious. In this regard, the Administration might wish to consider a country such as Paraguay. Paraguay's worker rights and human rights practices have long been recognized by the international human rights community, and even by the Reagan Administration, as among the worst in the world.[153] Paraguay moreover, is not a signatory to GATT and is thus not entitled to MFN treatment under the Agreement. While the imposition of trade sanctions under Section 301 against Paraguay would not guarantee any visible improvement in Paraguayan labor practices, such an action would send a clear message to the international community that the United States is ready to resume its leadership role in the struggle to promote worker rights and human rights abroad, and is prepared to use its economic resources aggressively to promote these goals.

---

153. *See* 1987 STATE DEP'T COUNTRY REPORTS, *supra* note 63, at 580-585; USTR GSP GENERAL REVIEW, *supra* note 56, at 5 (discussing Paraguayan labor practices).

IV. THE INTERNATIONAL EMERGENCY ECONOMIC POWERS ACT

A. The President's Authority Under the International Emergency Economic Powers Act

The International Emergency Economic Powers Act[154] (IEEPA) gives the President discretionary authority to impose trade restrictions on foreign countries when the acts, practices or policies of their governments create an . . .

> unusual and extraordinary threat, which has its source in whole or substantial part outside the United States, to the national security, foreign policy, or economy of the United States.[155]

To exercise his authority under the IEEPA, the President must declare a national emergency with respect to such a threat.[156] Such a declaration is necessary to remain consistent with GATT which creates an exception to the MFN clause in cases where a signatory's national security is imperiled by the actions of another signatory.[157]

B. The South African Sanctions

In 1985, the Reagan Administration invoked the IEEPA against the government of South Africa, in part due to that government's suppression of worker rights. On September 9, 1985, President Reagan formally declared "that the policies and actions of the Government of South Africa constitute an unusual and extraordinary threat to the foreign policy and economy of the United States and [I] hereby declare a national emergency to

---

154. Pub. L. No. 95-223, Title II, 91 Stat. 1626 (1977), codified at 50 U.S.C.A. § 1701 *et seq.* (West Supp. 1988) [hereinafter IEEPA].

155. 50 U.S.C.A. § 1701(a).

156. *Id.*

157. *See* GATT, *supra* note 18, Art. 21.

deal with that threat."[158] Section One of the President's order prohibited certain commercial transactions between U.S. citizens and South African governmental agencies including the export of computers, computer software, goods or technology relating to a nuclear production or utilization facility, arms, ammunition, or military vehicles to South Africa.[159] The President also prohibited U.S. citizens from making or approving certain loans to the South African government.[160]

Section Two of the President's order addressed the rights and welfare of South African workers. The order prohibited any agency of the U.S. government from assisting any foreign government with the export marketing activity of any U.S. national employing more than twenty-five workers in South Africa who did not adhere to seven basic principles concerning worker rights. The principles incorporated by the order were as follows:

> 1. Desegregating the races in each employment facility;
>
> 2. Providing equal employment opportunity for all employees without regard to race or ethnic origin;
>
> 3. Assuring that the pay system is applied to all employees without regard to race or ethnic origin;
>
> 4. Establishing a minimum wage and salary structure based on the appropriate local minimum economic level which takes into account the needs of employees and their families;
>
> 5. Increasing by appropriate means the number of persons in managerial, supervisory, administrative, clerical, and technical jobs who are disadvantaged by the apartheid system for the purpose of

---

158. Exec. Order No. 12,532, 50 Fed. Reg. 36,861 (1985).

159. *Id.* at § 1(b)-(d).

160. *Id.* at § 1(a).

> significantly increasing their representation in such jobs;
>
> 6. Taking reasonable steps to improve the quality of employees' lives outside the work environment with respect to housing, transportation, schooling, recreation and health;
>
> 7. Implementing fair labor practices by recognizing the right of all employees, regardless of racial or other distinctions, to self-organization and to form, join, or assist labor organizations, freely and without penalty or reprisal, and recognizing the right to refrain from any such activity.[161]

The President extended the national emergency concerning South Africa on September 4, 1986 claiming that the actions and policies of the South African government continued to pose an unusual and extraordinary threat to the foreign policy and economy of the United States.[162] The President declared that "[a]dditional measures to deal with this threat will be considered upon the completion of consultations with key Allies on joint, effective measures to eliminate apartheid and encourage negotiations for peaceful change in South Africa."[163]

C. Conclusion and Recommendations

Many of the GATT-based concerns relating to the proper use of Section 301 to promote worker rights are similarly applicable to the use of IEEPA to promote those objectives. To date, every President that has invoked powers granted by IEEPA has been careful to formally declare a "state of emergency" before imposing sanctions under this statute. The declaration of emergency thus falls within the exception to the GATT obligation of non-discriminatory tariff treatment under Article 21, at least on paper. A United States government assertion that the internal labor practices of a foreign

---

161. *Id.*

162. Notice of the President, 51 Fed. Reg. 31,925 (1986).

163. *Id.*

government created an "unusual and extraordinary threat" to the United States' national security, economy, or foreign policy would surely be challenged if the next Administration were to invoke IEEPA powers to sanction a fellow GATT signatory on the basis of worker rights violations.

Notwithstanding these concerns, the next Administration could use IEEPA to make an example of any one of a small number of countries, including GATT signatories such as Chile, Haiti or Romania, that commit the most flagrant worker rights and human rights violations. Since Article 22 of GATT allows each signatory to take appropriate trade action in times of national emergency, a government such as Chile's that sought to contest an IEEPA action at the GATT would be compelled to debate the merits of the United States' allegations concerning Chilean worker rights practices before a GATT panel. The Chilean government may be unprepared to subject itself to international scrutiny concerning its worker rights practices and might in that event merely accede to the United States' action under IEEPA. While such an undertaking might accomplish very little in terms of the worker rights practices of IEEPA targets, it would give the United States an opportunity to take a strong moral stand against the worst violators of internationally recognized worker rights.

LAWYERS COMMITTEE FOR HUMAN RIGHTS

STAFF

MICHAEL H. POSNER
Executive Director

WILLIAM G. O'NEILL
Deputy Director

ARTHUR C. HELTON
Director, Political Asylum Project

PATRICIA ARMSTRONG
1988 Project Coordinator

JOHN ASSADI
Staff Attorney

RAYMOND BROWN
Office Services

MARTHA L. DOGGETT
Human Rights Program

MARYAM ELAHI
Human Rights Internship Program

MIGDALIA GLORIA
Secretary

MITCHELL HARTMAN
Volunteer Projects
Coordinator

TERRY HUTCHINSON
Records Manager

MARIE JEANNOT
Executive Assistant

JULIE A. LYNCH
Legal Assistant

MAKAU MUTUA
Staff Attorney

MARTHA R. MOFFETT
Staff Attorney

SANDRA MORENO
Staff Attorney

MARGARET NICHOLSON
Director of Operations

VIRGINIA PETERS
Executive Assistant

PAMELA PRICE
Coordinator, Lawyer-to-
Lawyer Project

JEMERA RONE
Central America Representative
(Part-time)

JAMES D. ROSS
Staff Attorney

VIRGINIA SHERRY
Human Rights Program

WALTER WEISS
Staff Attorney